THE CULTIVATION OF
FERNS

THE CULTIVATION OF
FERNS

Andrew MacHugh

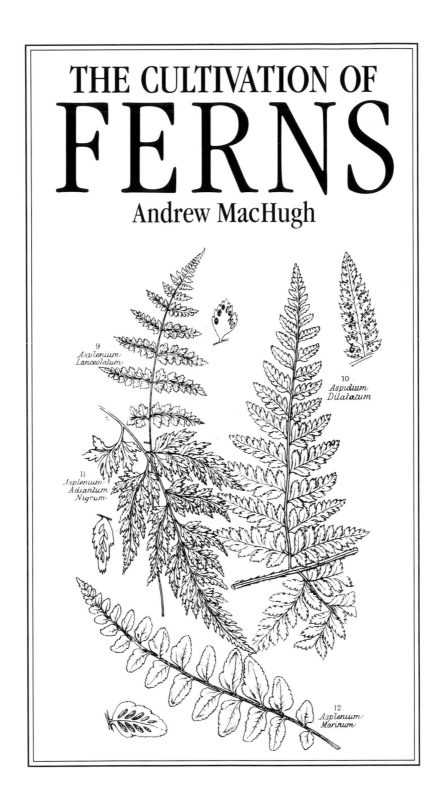

9
Asplenium
Lanceolatum

10
Aspidium
Dilatatum

11
Asplenium
Adiantum
Nigrum

12
Asplenium
Marinum

B.T. Batsford Ltd · London

ISBN 0 7134 6492 5

A catalogue entry for this title is available from the British Library
Typeset by J&L Composition Ltd, Filey, North Yorkshire
Printed
in Hong Kong
for the Publisher
B.T. Batsford Ltd
4 Fitzhardinge Street
London
W1H 0AH

CONTENTS

LIST OF COLOUR ILLUSTRATIONS

(between p. 64 and 65)

ACKNOWLEDGEMENTS

I wish to thank the staff and curators of the gardens which feature in this book. I am particularly indebted to Malcolm Hutcheson of Sizergh Castle, Daan Smit of the Free University of Amsterdam Botanic Garden and Leslie Bisset of Dundee Botanic Garden. Special thanks are extended to Jennifer Jones, whose valued comments, criticism and encouragement did much to lighten the burdens of authorship.

All photographs are by Andrew MacHugh and are reproduced by kind permission of the following: Dundee University Botanic Garden, plates 23, 25, 28, 29; Cheshire County Council, back cover, plates 26, 27, 38; Manchester Recreational Services, front cover, plates 1–3, 20–2, 30, 31, 37, 43; Manchester University, plate 24; National Trust, plates 4–13, 32–3, 35, 40, 42, 48; and The Northern Horticultural Society, plates 14–19, 34, 37, 39.

The illustrations on the title-page, and on pages 12, 22, 57, 61, 65, 71, 76, 89, and 95 are from the Rev. Edwin Bosanquet's *A Plain Account of British Ferns*, 1854. Line drawings on pages 21, 26, 84, 98–100, 103, 109, and 110 by Frances Oliver.

POPULAR FERNS AND THEIR COMMON NAMES

Adiantum capillus-veneris (maidenhair fern)
A. hispidulum (rosy maidenhair)
Anemia adiantifolia (pine fern)
A. phyllitidis (flowering fern)
Asplenium adiantum-nigrum (black spleenwort)
A. bulbiferum (mother and child fern)
A. nidus (bird's nest fern)
A. ruta-muraria (wall rue)
A. platyneuron (ebony spleenwort)
A. trichomanes subsp. quadrivalens (common maidenhair spleenwort)
A. trichomanes subsp. trichomanes (delicate maidenhair spleenwort)
A. viride (green spleenwort)
Athyrium distentifolium syn A. alpestre (alpine lady fern)
A. filix-femina (woodland lady fern)
A. flexile (flexile lady fern)
A. nipponicum 'pictum' (Japanese painted fern)
A. thelyptroides (silver glade fern)
Blechnum spicant (hard fern/deer fern)
B. occidentale (hammock fern)
Camptosorus rhizophyllus (walking fern)
Ceterach officinarum (rusty-back fern)
Cibotium barometz (Scythian lamb fern)
Cheilanthes lanosa (hairy lip fern)
Cryptogramma crispa (parsley fern)
Cyathea arbora (West Indian tree fern)
C. dealbata syn Alsophyla tricolor (silver tree fern)
Cyrtomium falcatum (Japanese holly fern)
Cystopteris fragilis (brittle bladder fern)
Davallia canariensis (hare's foot fern)
Dennstaedtia punctilobula (hay-scented fern)
Dicksonia antarctica (soft tree fern)
Drynaria quercifolia (oak-leaf fern)
Dryopteris aemula (hay-scented buckler fern)
D. affinis (golden-scaled male fern)
D. carthusiana (narrow buckler fern)
D. cristata (fen buckler fern)
D. dilatata (broad buckler fern)
D. expansa (Northern buckler fern)
D. filix-mas (common male fern)
D. goldiana (Goldie's fern/giant wood fern)

D. oreades (mountain male fern)
D. submontana (limestone buckler-fern)
Gymnocarpium dryopteris (woodland oak fern)
G. robertianum (limestone oak fern)
Hemionitis palmata (strawberry fern)
Humata tyermanii (hare's foot fern)
Hymenophyllum tunbrigense (Tunbridge filmy fern)
H. wilsonii (Wilson's filmy fern)
Lygodium japonicum (Japanese climbing fern)
L. palmatum (Hartford fern)
Matteuccia struthiopteris (shuttlecock fern/ostrich feather fern)
Nephrolepis cordifolia (fishbone fern/ladder fern)
Onoclea sensibilis (sensitive fern)
Onychium japonicum (Japanese claw fern)
Ophioglossum vulgatum (adder's tongue)
Oreopteris limbosperma (sweet mountain fern)
Osmunda cinnamomea (cinnamon fern)
O. Claytonia (interrupted fern)
O. regalis (royal fern)
Pellae atropurpurea (purple rock brake)
P. rotundifolia (button fern)
Phegopteris connectilis (beech fern)
Phyllitis scolopendrium (hart's tongue fern)
Pityrogramma argentea (goldback fern)
P. calomelanos (silver fern)
P. triangularis (California gold fern)
Platycerium elephantotis (elephant's ear fern)
P. bifurcatum (stag's horn fern)
Polypodium aureum (golden polypody)
P. australe (southern polypody)
P. glycyrrhiza (liquorice fern)
P. interjectum (Western polypody)
P. polypodioides (resurrection fern)
P. scouleri (leather fern)
P. vulgare (common polypody)
Polystichum acrostichoides (Christmas fern/dagger fern)
P. aculeatum (hard shield-fern)
P. lonchitis (holly fern)
P. setiferum (soft shield fern)
P. munitum (Western sword fern/giant holly fern)
Pteridium aquilinum (bracken)
Pteris cretica (ribbon fern)
P. ensiformis (sword brake fern)
P. serrulata (spider fern)
P. tremula (table fern)
Pyrrosia lingua (Japanese felt fern)
Salvinea minima (water spangles)
Tectaria cicutaria (button fern)
Thelypteris palustris (marsh fern)
T. hexagonoptera (broad beech fern)
Trichomanes speciosum (Killarney fern)
Woodwardia areolata (netted chain fern)

12

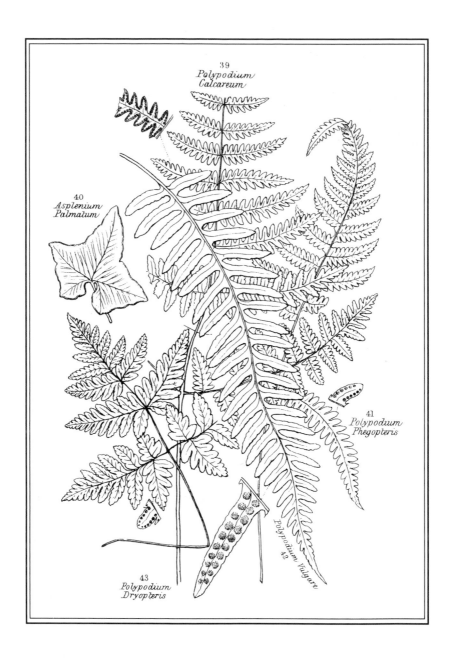

39
*Polypodium
Calcareum*

40
*Asplenium
Palmatum*

41
*Polypodium
Phegopteris*

*Polypodium vulgare
42*

43
*Polypodium
Dryopteris*

1
THE NINETEENTH-CENTURY HERITAGE

In recent years there has been a revival of interest in native plant species. Long neglected in favour of exotic hybrids, indigenous plants are being re-evaluated by today's gardeners and, in increasing numbers, our gardens are reflecting the understated charm and grace of the rich heritage of plants that make up the native flora.

No plants are more worthy of this renewed interest than the ferns. Though to the casual glance many species may look alike, closer inspection rewards the interested observer with a myriad of close resemblances and subtle differences between particular species. The most recent survey of fern populations lists 67 species native to Northern Europe (Page C.N. 1988). Temperate North America is host to 250 species. In addition to this wealth of species, the ferns' ability to hybridize has produced many distinct sub-species and varieties – a feature which proved a fascination to Victorian plant collectors. At the height of the 'Victorian Fern Craze', hundreds of fern varieties were discovered and named. Many more were systematically propagated and cultivated by enthusiasts keen to create more beautiful or novel forms.

Ironically, the Victorians' passion for these plants was a significant factor in reducing populations of ferns throughout Britain. During the 1850s and 1860s, gangs of fern hunters ranged the countryside uprooting rare and common species alike to satisfy town gardeners and collectors. As a consequence whole districts were denuded of fern species. *Osmunda regalis*, the royal fern, now protected by law, was one of many species to suffer virtual extinction as a wild plant.

At the turn of the eighteenth century there was little indication that native ferns would come to dominate the activities of a future generation of botanists and gardeners. There had existed collections of exotic ferns in Britain from as early as 1628, and the return of Bligh's 'Providence' in 1793 with 37 species from the West Indies stimulated further interest. However, in the absence of propagating techniques these collections remained small, relying upon overseas shipment, with its attendant expense and uncertainties, to maintain or increase stocks.

When James Bolton published *Filices Britannicae* in 1785, this first monograph on British ferns met with little response. Originally a weaver, the

Halifax publican, engraver and self-taught botanist was among the first to collect native ferns. Several decades later, Bolton's book, with its accurate illustrations by the author, offered a field guide to an emerging band of fern collectors and was to be the model for many of the fern books of the following century.

Among the first to understand the complexities of the fern's reproductive cycle was the surgeon and botanist John Lindsay. Whilst living in Jamaica, Lindsay had become fascinated by the abundance and diversity of ferns growing in that region and, for eight years from 1786, he applied himself to experimenting in fern propagation. In 1794, with the support of the eminent botanist Sir John Banks, Lindsay's account of raising ferns from spores was reported to the Linnean Society of London, founded some 14 years earlier by James Edward Smith. Published in the prestigious journal of the Linnean Society, Lindsay's discoveries were widely read and provided the spur to further experiments in Britain and other parts of Europe.

With the understanding of fern propagation came the first impetus towards more widespread popularity. By the second decade of the nineteenth century some of the principal elements were in place that would thrust ferns to dizzy heights of popularity in succeeding decades.

John Shepherd, the first curator of Liverpool Botanic Garden, was among the first to capitalize on Lindsay's work. Within the space of a few years from its creation in 1803, the garden had gained a respected reputation for its collection of exotic and native fern species. Interest in Shepherd's work with ferns spread to other botanic gardens and private estates. By the 1840s there were notable collections of ferns in various public gardens. John Smith had built up extensive collections of ferns at the Royal Botanic Garden, Edinburgh and later developed an enviable collection at Kew. David Cameron, curator of Birmingham Botanic Garden, had established a notable collection of British and exotic ferns. However, the richest collections were in the hands of a few private collectors: Robert Barklay of Dorking, Surrey, who had for a time David Cameron as his head gardener, had amassed an impressive range of native British species, and John Riley of Papplewick, Nottinghamshire had by the time of his death in 1847 some 300 species and varieties.

However, wih the exception of a few individuals, the main focus of interest, until the 1830s, was in exotic species cultivated in the stove houses of the public gardens and large estates. About this time, a further increase in fern enthusiasm arose as a result of the widening interest in botany, and prompted a shift of emphasis to native species.

Under the guidance of James Edward Smith, who introduced the Linnean system of plant classification to Britain, botany emerged as a fashionable pursuit among the court of George III. By the time the young Queen Victoria had acceded to the throne, an understanding of the plant world had become a valued accomplishment among the upper middle classes. A wide assortment of manuals, from the learned to the sentimental, offered instruction in this most fashionable of pursuits. By the end of the century the hobby had percolated throughout British society so pervasively, few individuals were left untouched by the lure of botanizing.

In the climate of botanical inquisitiveness that characterized the age, natural history societies had been formed in many industrial cities and towns. These largely middle-class institutions had their counterpart in the informal field clubs of working men and women who ventured beyond the factories and mills on Sunday rambles. This network of amateur botanists was sustained by a range of natural history and horticultural journals which were launched between 1800 and 1840. In the pages of these publications the first flush of popular interest in native ferns can be detected.

It was John Loudon's *The Gardener's Magazine* which first publicized, in 1834, the use of closed glass cases to house ferns. Invented by Nathaniel Ward, an indomitable student of natural history and fern collector, its primary use was to house a hawk moth chrysalis. Within the confines of the case the spores of *Dryopteris filix-mas* had germinated and prospered in the humid atmosphere. Having despaired of cultivating ferns within the inhospitable environs of London's Whitechapel, his chance discovery encouraged Ward to design further cases for the experimental cultivation of a variety of fern species. Rather surprisingly, Ward's success with some 60 species of ferns did not move him to publicize his achievements. Were it not for the enthusiasm of Loudon and Ward's fellow members in the Linnean Society, this revolutionary discovery might have languished in obscurity. As later events proved, Ward's glazed case was to inspire a radical transformation in Victorian interiors and to help foster fern enthusiasm among a wider sphere of society.

With the discovery of the Ward case, botany came indoors. Ward's invention, together with new glassmaking techniques pioneered by Robert Chance and the abolition of the glass tax in 1845, signalled a new era in gardening practice. The fumes from gas lighting, coal fires and industrial pollution had, until the innovation of the Ward case, made the cultivation of plants indoors impossible. Within a few years of Ward's discovery no middle-class home was to be without its glazed case. Manufacturers rushed to satisfy the demand, outdoing each other with the elaborateness of their designs.

If the humblest home was not to be without its Ward case, the more affluent elements of society sought to mirror the glass structures now being assembled in private parks and in the botanic gardens of the industrial cities and towns. The great conservatory at Chatsworth (1836), the Palm House, Kew (1844), the Winter Garden, Regent's Park (1846), Crystal Palace (1850) and Lord Egerton's conservatory at Tatton (1852) brought gardening, and fern cultivation, to new levels of popularity. The conservatory became an essential feature of suburban villas. Here, with the help of such books as Loudon's *The Suburban Gardener and Villa Companion* (1838), the fruits of botanizing trips could be cultivated, observed and catalogued. With increasing prosperity and a developing railway network, field trips became a familiar family pursuit for the middle classes, the spoils of their endeavours being brought back in hampers and planted up in the indoor garden, or dried and pressed for the herbarium.

Ferns were the ideal subjects for these amateur botanists. The ferns' growing period allowed fruitful excursions to be undertaken from spring to autumn. The wealth of species available was a further attraction in an age which was obsessed with collections of all kinds. A day's fern hunting could furnish some 20 species if the location was carefully chosen.

However, it was the aesthetic appeal of the ferns which prompted such widespread botanic activity. In a society which was increasingly being blighted by the effects of industrialization, the cool green symmetry of the ferns conjured the sylvan charm of a romanticized rural past. In suburban conservatories, and in their miniaturized counterpart, the Ward case, the Victorians could evoke arcadian retreats. More ambitious fern enthusiasts sculpted grottoes and elaborate rock works to create fantastical gardenscapes.

It was into this favourable milleu that the fern books were launched. George William Francis' *An Analysis of British Ferns and their Allies* (1837) provided detailed descriptions and specific locations of fern sites together with illustrations by the author. Francis' knowledge of ferns was gained initially whilst he was an apprentice at the respected Hackney nursery firm of Loggiges. From Francis' book it was obvious that a well developed chain of correspondence had already been in existence for some years. His observations were compiled with the help of the first flush of amateur botanists and fern collectors. A slim volume of 70 pages, its compact size and its detailed descriptions of species helped make the ferns accessible to the growing band of field botanists.

One of the most influential fern books emerged just three years after Francis' *An Analysis of British Ferns and their Allies*. Edward Newman's *A History of British Ferns* (1840) was widely acclaimed in the botanical journals. On its publication *The Magazine of Natural History* announced, 'To every lover of British Botany we cordially recommend Mr. Newman's volume'. Acknowledging the wider participation of women in the pursuit, Loudon's *The Gardener's Magazine* recommended it as, 'A valuable present to the lady botanist', a sentiment echoed in *The Gardener's Chronicle and Agricultural Gazette*'s claim that the book was one 'No lady ought to be without'. Perhaps the most impressive testimony for the book came from Ward himself. 'Those who are desirous of acquiring acquaintance with our native species of this beautiful and interesting order of plants', he wrote, 'cannot do better than consult Mr. Newman's *History of British Ferns*'.

With the publication of the books by Francis and Newman, together with the fourth volume of Richard Deakin's *Florographia Britannicae* (1841) which was devoted to ferns, the momentum of fern collecting increased. By the mid 1840s Thomas Moore, the man who, above all others, was to dominate the world of ferns, had gone into print with *A Handbook of British Ferns*. Moore had extended his observations to fern varieties. Barely mentioned in Francis' *An Analysis of British ferns*, these were by now the preoccupation of the field botanists. Newman revised his *A History of British Ferns* in 1845 to cater for this shift of emphasis, noting varietal forms as well as cultivation hints. However, it was Moore who was unsurpassed in providing full descriptions of the then known varieties, with detailed locations and coloured illustrations by Fitch. Moore's *British Ferns* (1851) became the bible of the fern collectors and a stimulus for a new wave of fern enthusiasts.

Although Francis, Newman and Moore were the acclaimed authorities throughout this period many, more minor, figures contributed to the fern literature. Between 1840 and 1866, 20 field guides on ferns were published.

Whilst the fern books brought fresh devotees to the pursuit, they helped to make it all too easy for the less principled to exploit the vogue. By the mid 1860s hostility was being expressed in the press against commercial fern collectors. Employing youths to scour the countryside, they hawked their cartloads of ferns on the streets of the industrial towns, selling their wares to those reluctant to make their own excursions. The commercial exploitation of native populations was both wasteful and unnecessary. Most of the uprooted ferns did not survive the clumsy handling and poor storage on their journey from countryside to town. The inexperience of the hawkers made them oblivious to the value of their plants and indifferent to the damage they inflicted on fern populations.

The emergence of collection on a commercial scale signalled a new development. Until the end of the 1860s field trips were the major source of fern collections. Whether through depletion of fern habitats or as a result of changing fashion, emphasis turned to fern growing. James Shirley Hibbert's *The Fern Garden: How to Make, Keep and Enjoy It* (1869) went to eight editions over ten years. It was Hibbert's *Rustic Adornments for Homes of Taste* (1856) which had so eloquently fostered the popular taste for indoor ferneries. *The Fern Garden* brought a new sector of the public to fern cultivation. Previously the preserve of the middle class, Hibbert's book encouraged the less affluent to turn their small, town gardens to fern cultivation.

Partly through satiation, partly through a certain sense of snobbery, the middle classes, now that ferns had become the hobby of the 'lower orders', turned from ferns to collecting the exotic plants now entering Britain from the far reaches of the Empire. Necessarily expensive to obtain, their price conferred a cachet on their owners and provided an adequate reflection of social standing.

Along with the entry of a new public keen to take up fern cultivation, but without the resources of time, money or skill to obtain their plants from the field, emerged a new breed of nurserymen specializing in ferns. Until the 1850s there had only been a handful of fern nurserymen who were, in the main, originally collectors who had drifted into the trade.

Throughout the first half of the nineteenth century the Hackney nurserymen, Loggiges and Sons, had been at the forefront of fern cultivation. Benefiting from Lindsay's experiments, Loggiges were the first to propagate ferns on a commercial scale. By 1818 Loggiges had 33 hardy and 14 exotic species of fern in their catalogue. A keen plantsman and astute businessman,

George Loggiges published his catalogue in two volumes, with notes on correct cultivation together with handsome illustrations by G. Cook. *The Botanical Cabinet*, 1817–18, was succeeded by a monthly subscription magazine, again with illustrations by Cook. By the 1850s the firm was finding a wider market for their ferns among a growing band of collectors. Responding to this demand, other nurseries were springing up around the country. Robert Sim, of Kray's Foot, Kent, could boast 818 species and varieties of ferns. Abraham Stansfield, initially a private collector, offered 50 varieties of *Phyllitis scolopendrium* (hart's tongue) in his catalogue of 1840. By 1862, his catalogue contained 1,100 species and varieties. John Lloyd, again originally a collector, and William Pamplin, both of Wandsworth, had extensive numbers of ferns in their catalogues.

The 1870s witnessed a proliferation of fern nurseries, most specializing in native species. Although 'fern mania' had abated by this time there was still sufficient interest in these species to support the 20 or more large firms who continued to supply a buoyant market until the onset of the First World War. Among the largest was W. & J. Birkenhead of Sale, Cheshire. Their 1875 catalogue listed some 2,000 species and varieties. Other significant nurseries included W.F. Askew of Grange, Borrowdale, James Blackhouse of York, who specialized in filmy ferns, Edmund Gill of Lynton, Devon, with a catalogue listing 1,000 species and varieties, Robert Kennedy of Covent Garden, London, and Henry B. May of Upper Edmunton.

The 1870s also saw the last significant chapter of fern cultivation. Until that time it had been considered impossible for hybridization to occur between species. When in 1868 E.J. Lowe set out before the British Association for the Advancement of Science the results of his successful experiments in hybridization little credence was given to his work. Lowe's discoveries were not acknowledged by the new breed of professional botanists until the publication of *Fern Growing* (1895), in which Lowe detailed the results of many thousands of experiments in hybridization conducted by himself and other enthusiasts, including Major Brett Cowburn of Dennel Hill, South Wales, Edwin Fox of Bristol, Colonel Arthur Jones of Clifton, Bristol and John Mapplewick of Dolgellau, North Wales.

The great fern collectors of the 1830s and 1840s, such as Walter C. Trevelyan, W.H. Allchin, Robert Barklay, and John Riley nurtured the Victorian public's affection for the ferns and set a trend that was to occupy a nation's activities for several decades. The later contribution of Lowe and his colleagues was equally significant, bringing forth a wealth of new varieties to enrich and adorn gardens and interiors.

Sadly, between the turn of the century and the present day there has been a great loss of fern varieties. The large country estates which were the sites of fern experimentation and cultivation have long since been broken up and their plant collections lost. Financial constraints on the botanic gardens of the universities and the public parks, in many cases the recipients of bequests of fern collections, have further diminished the Victorian collectors' heritage.

In the wild, the range and distribution of almost all fern species have declined, to the extent that those which once were widespread are now confined to diminishing and isolated sites. Much of this is due to the extensive changes that have taken place in the environment since the Victorians made their fern surveys. The loss of plant habitats due to industrial development, in the form of road-making and building construction, together with changed agricultural practices, has pushed fern populations increasingly back to isolated, marginal land. Hedges, verges and copses have disappeared wholesale. Wetlands, woodlands and limestone areas – typically host to the majority of ferns – have seen the greatest changes as communities and technology have exploited previously underdeveloped land.

While there is little chance of fern populations returning to pre-Victorian levels, the increasing focus on ecological issues offers the opportunity to stem the decline of existing habitats. The creation of conservation areas and country parks, together with the rising popularity of native plant species in garden schemes, provide some locations where the neglect of fern species can be reversed.

Although the fate of native wild species is at present uncertain there is no mistaking the ferns' increasing popularity both as garden subjects and house plants. It seems that now the ferns are rapidly emerging from the neglect and near-oblivion into which they have been cast since their halcyon days of the last century. Their unrivalled diversity of form and richness of foliage can enhance the most unpromising situation, lending exotic charm to the most mundane.

2
CHARACTERISTICS OF THE FERN FAMILIES

The ferns are an ancient group of plants, evolving some 350,000,000 years ago. The success of ferns in evolutionary terms is indicated by the geographical diversity of their habitats, extending from the frozen wastes of Alaska to the tropical jungles of the equatorial rainforests. Their variety of form is equally impressive, ranging from the tiny *Marsilea quadrifolia* (water shamrock) which grows from 3–6in. (8–16cm) in Australian marshland to the impressive *Dicksonia antarctica* (soft tree fern), another Australian species, which grows to 50ft (14.6m) in the tropical upland forests of Queensland.

CLASSIFICATION

Since the days of the Victorian amateur fern-hunters, botanists have sought to establish a satisfactory classificatory scheme for fern species. Even today there remains much academic dispute over the classification of the 12,000 species that compose the world-wide fern population.

Traditionally, the difficulties involved in fern identification and classification have dissuaded many gardeners from pursuing an interest in these fascinating plants. However, an aversion to botanical terms need not prevent the individual from cultivating these intriguing and versatile plants. As much, if not more, can be learned from first-hand observation in the garden and greenhouse as from learned technical volumes.

Ferns (pteridophytes) are classified under four headings of descending generality: family, genus, species, and variety.

Most authorities recognize 30 families into which the world-wide genera of ferns are grouped. One family, Athyriaceae, for example, contains seven genera – *Adenoderris*, *Athyrium*, *Cystopteris*, *Diplazium*, *Gymnocarpium*, *Hemidictyum* and *Woodsia*.

Within the genus *Athyrium* are some 100 species. The six most commonly cultivated are *A. australe*, *A. distentifolium* (alpine lady fern), *A. filix-femina* (woodland lady fern), *A. flexile* (flexile lady fern), *A. nipponicum* and *A. pynocarpon* (glade fern). A further division is possible into distinct varieties of particular species. The species *Athyrium filix-femina* has a particularly large number of varieties in cultivation including *Athyrium filix-femina minutissimum* – a miniature lady fern 4–6in. (10–16cm) in height, *Athyrium filix-femina plumosum percristatum* – a very attractive crested form and *A.f.f. Victoriae*, a natural variety found in a wayside lane in Ayrshire, Scotland, in the last century.

FAMILY ATHYRIACEAE

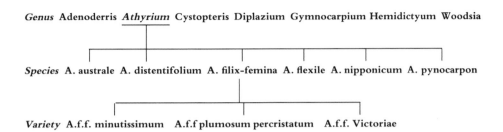

Genus Adenoderris *Athyrium* Cystopteris Diplazium Gymnocarpium Hemidictyum Woodsia

Species A. australe A. distentifolium A. filix-femina A. flexile A. nipponicum A. pynocarpon

Variety A.f.f. minutissimum   A.f.f plumosum percristatum   A.f.f. Victoriae

COMPONENT PARTS OF A FERN

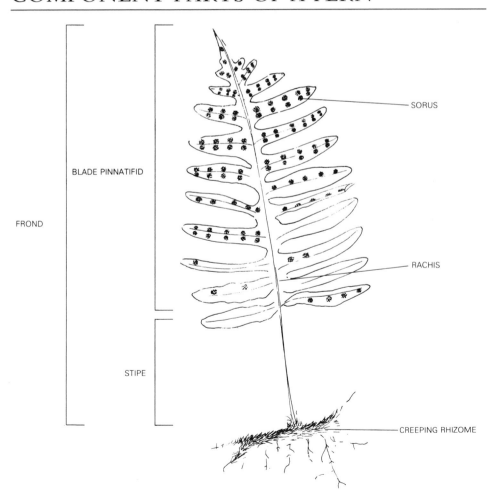

FROND

BLADE PINNATIFID

STIPE

SORUS

RACHIS

CREEPING RHIZOME

In common with the flowering plants the foliage of the fern, the frond, provides the plant with its means of photosynthesis. In addition, the fronds bear clusters of spores (sori) which are the mechanisms of reproduction. In some genera, such as *Blechnum* and *Osmunda*, a separate set of fronds bears the spores. In other genera the spores are carried on the undersides of mature fronds. When the spores ripen, varying according to species from July to September, the protective covering of scale (indusium) breaks open to release the microscopic spores.

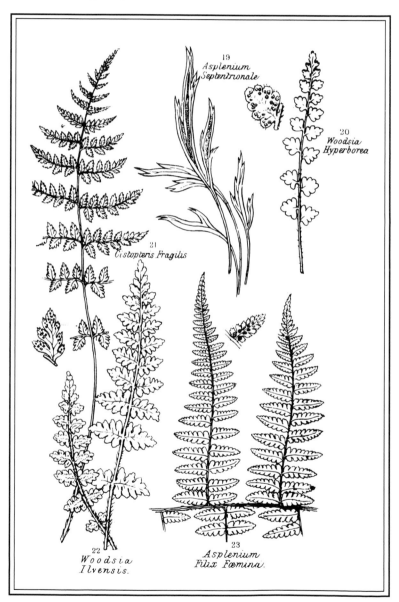

In keeping with the vast range of fern species, the architecture of ferns encompasses a diverse range of forms. Even among the 300 species of temperate Europe and America there are a wide range of frond forms.

The simplest form of frond is that of *Asplenium scolopendrium* (hart's tongue fern) and *Camptosorus rhizophyllus* (strap fern). Here the frond is made up of stem (stipe) and strap-like blade bisected by the mid–rib (rachis). In late summer the underside of the blade bears the sori enclosed in linear indusia.

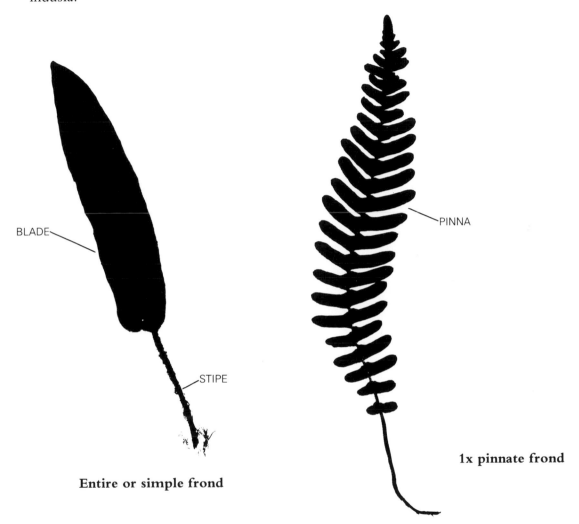

BLADE

STIPE

Entire or simple frond

PINNA

1x pinnate frond

While this type of simple frond architecture can be found also in epiphytic ferns of tropical regions, it is untypical. Most ferns display a much greater degree of segmentation of the frond blade, the simplest being a division either side of the mid rib as in *Ceterach officinarum* (rusty back fern) and *Polypodium vulgare* (common polypody). In both of these species the division on either side does not reach the mid rib and the shape is described as pinnatifid.

In the case of *Blechnum spicant* (hard fern), where the division extends to the mid rib, giving the appearance of a herringbone outline, its fronds are termed pinnate, each section of the herringbone being a pinna.

2x pinnate frond

PINNULES

A more complex structure is exhibited by *Dryopteris filix-mas* (common male fern), *Cystopteris fragilis* (brittle bladder fern) and *Polystichum aculeatum* (hard shield fern). These are 2× pinnate, or bipinnate, having a further division of each pinna. These secondary divisions are pinnules. *Athyrium filix-femina* (lady fern), *Adiantum capillus-veneris* (maidenhair fern) and *Cryptogramma crispa* (parsley fern), which are further divided on their secondary pinnae, are 3× pinnate, or tripinnate.

Once this system of classification is adopted in the observation of ferns, identification of species can be surprisingly swiftly mastered.

A further aid to identification of species can be gained by observing the shape of the sori. The sori of *Athyrium filix-femina* have a 'J' or 'C'-shaped indusia. The *Dryopteris* species have sori enclosed within kidney-shaped indusia. *Polystichum aculeatum* (hard shield fern), *P. setiferum* (soft shield fern) and *P. lonchitis* (holly fern) enclose sori within circular indusia. In *Phyllitis scolopendrium* and *Asplenium* species the sori is enclosed within linear indusia.

The rootstock, or rhizome, in conjunction with frond outlines and the shape of the indusium often will provide a guide to identification.

Erect, trunk-forming rhizomes are typical of some tropical species including *Cyathea*, *Dicksonia*, and *Diplazium*. Under ideal conditions these ferns reach tree-like proportions.

Long, creeping rhizomes are characteristic of tropical epiphytes such as *Lygodium*, *Microsorium*, *Humata* and *Davallia*. Hardy species of temperate regions with this rhizome form include *Polypodium*, a successful colonizer of man-made walls and brickwork, *Gymnocarpium dryopteris* (oak fern), *Phegopteris connectilis* (beech fern) – both species of the open-textured acid woodland soils – and the rare, protected species of filmy ferns, including *Trichomanes speciosum* (Killarney fern), whose natural habitat is the water-washed acidic boulders of streamside banks and ravines.

Short, decumbent rhizomes typify *Adiantum*, *Cheilanthes*, *Cystopteris* and *Woodsia* species. Fronds arise from the rootstock in congested, often irregular, clusters. Generally colonizers of walls and rock clefts, their wiry roots allow purchase in moist and shady crevices.

Erect, ascending rhizomes, or crowns, send up fronds in the form of a shuttlecock, closely packed and symmetrical. As they develop over the years, the crowns gradually enlarge until they are clearly visible above the ground or amongst boulders. Typical of this habitat are *Athyrium*, *Asplenium*, *Dryopteris*, *Polystichum* and *Osmunda* species. In winter and early spring the new season's fronds at the centre of the crown are surrounded by the remains of the previous year's tissue.

Although the complexities of species identification may seem daunting, there is no doubt that systematic observation will overcome any initial mystification. For the successful cultivation of ferns the technical aspects of fern configuration are secondary to ensuring that soil and climatic factors match the needs of particular species. To this end chapter 3 outlines the native habitats of fern species. By offering fern species conditions which reflect those prevalent in the native habitat, success can be ensured.

THE FERN LIFE CYCLE

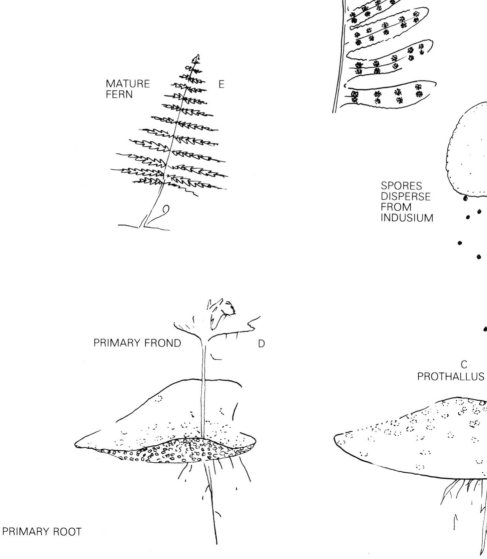

A   FERTILE FROND

MATURE FERN   E

B

SPORES DISPERSE FROM INDUSIUM

PRIMARY FROND   D

C
PROTHALLUS

PRIMARY ROOT

In view of its diversity of form and widespread distribution it is surprising that the reproductive system of the fern was not discovered until the last century. The mystery surrounding the fern life cycle seems to be responsible for the many myths which were associated in past ages with these plants. Indeed, their classification as cryptogams, meaning 'hidden fruiting', indicates the obscurity that veiled their reproductive system.

The ferns we see growing in the wild and in our gardens represent only one part of the fern life cycle. Unlike the flowering plants, ferns have no reproductive organs: sexual reproduction occurs at another stage in the fern life cycle. This process, unique to cryptogams, is known as the alternation of generations.

When fructification takes place, in summer and early autumn, tiny dust-like particles are produced on the back of the fronds (**A**). These spores are protected by scaly membranes or indusia. When the spores ripen the indusia break open and the spores are released (**B**). Many thousands of spores are released from a mature plant, but of these only a few will succeed to the next stage in the cycle.

Given suitable levels of humidity and light, the scattered individual spores will develop a chain of cells. Over a period of weeks these cells develop into a heart-shaped plant called a prothallus (**C**). The small organism, $\frac{1}{4}$in. (0.6cm) in size, is anchored to the soil by root-like rhizoids during this period.

This is the sexual stage of the fern cycle. Within the prothallus are male parts (antheridia) which contain the sperm, and female parts (archegonia) which contain the eggs. The presence of a film of moisture on the prothallus will allow the male sperm to swim across the prothallus and fertilize an egg.

Upon fertilization a further stage is initiated. The fertilized egg grows on the prothallus, developing into a new plant (**D**), which will eventually resemble the parent plant. Over a period of six months to a year the new plant draws nourishment from the prothallus. Eventually the prothallus will shrivel and disappear, as the new plant develops a separate root structure (**E**). The cycle from ripened spore to new plant may take from one to two years.

3
NATIVE FERN SPECIES AND THEIR HABITATS

Ferns are universally acknowledged as being among the loveliest of our native plants. The wayside lanes, woodland walks and streamside banks bear witness throughout spring and summer to the charm and vigour of these remarkable plants. Their pleasing symmetry of form and striking freshness of foliage capture our attention and delight our eye. In late summer and early autumn, expeditions into the countryside reward us with the mellow – and sometimes spectacular – beauty of the ferns' fading foliage, a riot of yellows, russets and browns – mirroring the canopy of leaf above.

It is not surprising that generations of gardeners and country lovers have attempted to bring to city and suburban plots a little of the wilderness so exemplified by the fern, as a reminder of more pleasurable locations. Sadly, their efforts have often not been crowned with success, and cherished ideas of emulating Nature have been dashed, with the early death of favourite specimens.

Generally, the failure of these cultivators lay in their ignorance of the ferns' requirements. Ferns are forgiving plants and will stand some lack of attention – indeed as wild plants they thrive on neglect. However, they will not survive the murderous effects of being planted in an alien environment lacking their particular basic needs of soil and exposure to sun. Success in bringing the radiance and delicacy of the fern into town and suburban gardens involves some understanding of the needs of particular ferns. A little knowledge of their native habitats, and directing cultivation with this in mind, will serve to avoid recreating the conditions one can observe in many town gardens, where stunted ferns struggle valiantly on unsuitable, impoverished sites.

Habitats vary according to five factors: climate, altitude, humidity, soil type and exposure to sun.

Whereas some ferns can be found in a range of habitats, others are local to one type of habitat. For example, *Dryopteris filix-mas* (male fern) and *Athyrium filix-femina* (lady fern) can be found in a range of habitats from sea-level marshland to hedgebank and mountainside, while *Ceterach officinarum* (rusty-back fern) is generally only to be found growing in the cracks of old mortared walls.

THE FERNS OF TEMPERATE EUROPE

Adiantum capillus-veneris (maidenhair fern), *Asplenium adiantum-nigrum* (black spleenwort), *Asplenium billotii* (lanceolate spleenwort), *A. marinum* (sea spleenwort), *A. ruta-muraria* (wall rue), *A. septentrionale*, *A. anopteris*, *A. trichomanes*, subsp. *quadrivalens* (common maidenhair spleenwort), *A. trichomanes*, subsp. *trichomanes* (delicate maidenhair spleenwort), *A. viride* (green spleenwort), *A.* x *alternifolium* (alternate-leaved spleenwort), *Athyrium distentifolium* syn *A. alpestre* (alpine lady fern), *Athyrium filix-femina* (lady fern), *A. flexile* (flexile lady fern), *Blechnum spicant* (hard fern), *Ceterach officinarum* (rusty-back fern), *Cryptogramma crispa* (parsley fern), *Cystopteris fragilis*, *C. dickieana*, *C. montana*, *Dryopteris aemula* (hay-scented buckler fern), *Dryopteris affinis* (golden-scaled male fern), *D. carthusiana* (narrow buckler fern), *D. cristata* (fen buckler fern), *D. dilatata* (broad buckler fern), *D. expansa* (northern buckler-fern), *D. filix-mas* (common male fern), *D. fragrans*, *D. oreades* (mountain fern), *D. submontana* (limestone buckler fern), *D.* x *deweveri* (hybrid buckler fern), *D.* x *mantoniae* (hybrid buckler fern), *Gymnocarpium dryopteris* (woodland oak fern), *Gymnocarpium robertianum* (limestone oak fern), *Hymenophyllum tunbrigense* (Tunbridge filmy fern), *Hymenophyllum wilsonii* (Wilsons filmy fern), *Matteuccia struthiopteris* (shuttlecock fern), *Oreopteris limbosperma* (sweet mountain-fern), *Osmunda regalis* (royal fern), *Phegopteris connectilis* (beech fern), *Phyllitis scolopendrium* (hart's tongue fern), *Polypodium australe* (Southern polypody), *Polypodium interjectum* (Western polypody), *P. vulgare* (common polypody), *Polystichum aculeatum* (hard shield fern), *P. braunii*, *Polystichum lonchitis* (holly fern), *P. setiferum* (soft shield-fern), *Pteridium aquilinum* (bracken), *Thelypteris palustris* (marsh fern), *Trichomanes speciosum* (Killarney fern), *Woodsia alpina* (alpine woodsia), *Woodsia ilvensis* (oblong woodsia), *W. galbella*.

Habitats

Forest and woodland

The best known habitats of ferns are forest and woodland. Most people are familiar with the ferns of the woodland, where high humidity and deep or dappled shade are the ideal conditions for the graceful and varied *Athyrium filix-femina* (lady fern). This of all the ferns offers the greatest variety of form and habit. It is possible to see several points of difference in a colony within the space of a few yards; indeed the difficulty is to spot which two are alike.

Alongside *Athyrium f.f.* can be found *Polystichum setiferum* (soft shield fern) together with two of the *Dryopteris* species, *Dryopteris carthusiana* (narrow buckler) and *D. dilatata* (broad buckler). Rather rarer inhabitants of this habitat are *Gymnocarpium dryopteris* (oak fern), with its beautiful triple-jointed fronds, and *Dryopteris aemula* (hay-scented buckler), which if bruised gives off a scent not unlike that of new-mown hay. Given some shade during the hottest part of the day and a soil which does not dry out, these ferns will lend beauty and charm to any garden.

Verges and hedgebanks

Along the wayside verges and hedgebanks in the more sparsely populated areas of the country, most of the ferns of the woodland prosper, together with *Phyllitis scolopendrium* (hart's tongue), whose strap-like fronds can grow to 18in. (46cm) in favourable conditions. Here also can be found, often in great numbers, the vigorous *Dryopteris filix-mas* (male fern), making clumps of individual plants up to 2ft (61cm) and 3ft (91cm) across.

On the more stony areas of hedgebanks can be found *Polypodium vulgare* (common polypody), creating an evergreen carpet. In spring, the sight of the fresh green fronds, emerging from beneath the darker green, partially-bronzed fronds of the previous year, hints at the arrival of summer.

Banks of rivers and streams

By the banks of rivers and streams the acidic, moist soil and high humidity creates ideal conditions for *A. filix-femina* (lady fern), *Polystichum setiferum* (soft shield fern) and the strange *Blechnum spicant* (hard fern), with its bright green, toothcomb-like fronds. This last-mentioned fern luxuriates in the spongy, peaty soil, high in acidity, which is to be found in this type of site.

Walls

The dry-stone and weathered mortared walls of the countryside offer a perfect habitat for those ferns which love to keep their roots moist and shaded. Here can be found, often in abundance, *Polypodium vulgare* (polypody), several species of *Asplenium* (spleenworts), *Phyllitis scolopendrium* (hart's tongue) and that most delicate of ferns – especially in spring and early summer when its fronds are the picture of bright green delicacy – *Cystopteris fragilis* (brittle bladder fern).

Mortared walls are also home to one of the most curious of ferns – *Ceterach officinarum* (rusty-back fern), aptly named, for its rippled fronds appear green on the upper surface and brown underneath. This is an evergreen fern, often making a dense carpet of fronds

Limestone crags

The limestone crags of the western seaboard of Northern Europe offer hospitable growing conditions to a range of ferns which thrive on a constant seepage of lime-rich moisture. Sheltering in the cracks and crannies which offer roots close contact with the rock face grow several forms of *Asplenium* (spleenwort), *Phyllitis scolopendrium* (hart's tongue), *Cystopteris fragilis* (brittle bladder fern) and *Polystichum lonchitis* (holly fern). Amongst the higher reaches of the crags, and more rarely seen, grows *Gymnocarpium robertianum* (limestone oak fern).

Marshland

Those marshlands and bogs which still remain can offer suitable conditions for some of the rarest ferns. These include *Osmunda regalis* (royal fern) – perhaps the most impressive European native species, in ideal conditions growing to 6ft (2m) in height and several feet broad. Here also can be found *Thelypteris palustris* (marsh fern), *Polystichum setiferum* (soft shield fern) and several *Dryopteris* species – including the extremely rare, *D. cristata* (fen-buckler fern) which throws up a crown of rigid vertical fronds in spring.

Sea cliffs

Another habitat of rare species are the sea cliffs in the West, where the diminishing populations of *Adiantum capillus-veneris* (maidenhair fern), *Asplenium marinum* (sea spleenwort) and *A. billotii* (lanceolate spleenwort) survive in the crannies and fissures of the rock face. These plants thrive on the combination of moisture-laden air and the mild Gulf Stream climate. They usually do not survive any outdoor situation inland which is not completely sheltered.

Moorland and mountain

Some of the rarest of Northern European ferns colonize the mountain-sides and high moorland. Rocky, limestone ledges and scree slopes offer shelter to alpine species, including *Athyrium distentifolium* syn. *A. alpestre* (alpine lady fern), *Phegopteris connectilis* (beech fern) – usually present near waterfalls, *Polystichum lonchitis* (holly fern), *P. aculeatum* (hard shield fern), *Oreopteris limbosperma* (sweet mountain fern) and *Cystopteris montana* (mountan bladder fern). Usually far from roads, these ferns are rarely seen by any, except walkers and climbers.

Many of the Northern European native species described above have developed distinct sub-species which have been named and taken into cultivation. Many of these forms are considered to be especially interesting. Those gardeners who take the trouble to seek them out in the catalogues of the specialist fern nurseries, or more ambitiously through their own sorties into fern propagation, will be rewarded by the beauty and delicacy of form that many of these rarities possess.

Species found in distinct habitats

The following outlines fern species to be found in distinct habitats. This can be used as a guide to matching available sites with suitable species of fern.

Woodland shade

Athyrium filix-femina (lady fern), *Adiantum capillus-veneris* (maidenhair fern),

Asplenium adiantum-nigrum (black spleenwort), *Dryopteris carthusiana* (narrow buckler fern), *Dryopteris aemula* (hay-scented buckler fern), *D. dilatata* (broad buckler fern), *D. filix-mas* (male fern), *Gymnocarpium dryopteris* (oak fern), *Polypodium vulgare* (common polypody), *Polystichum aculeatum* (hard shield fern), *Polystichum setiferum* (soft shield fern).

Hedgebanks

Athyrium filix-femina (lady fern), *Asplenium adiantum-nigrum* (black spleenwort), *Dryopteris affinis* (scaly male fern), *Dryopteris aemula* (hay-scented buckler), *D. dilatata* (broad buckler fern), *D. filix-mas* (male fern), *Phyllitis scolopendrium* (hart's tongue), *Polypodium vulgare* (common polypody), *Polystichum aculeatum* (hard shield fern), *Polystichum setiferum* (soft shield fern).

Riversides

Athyrium filix-femina (lady fern), *Blechnum spicant* (hard fern), *Dryopteris aemula* (hay-scented buckler), *Gymnocarpium dryopteris* (oak fern), *Matteuccia struthiopteris* (shuttlecock fern), *Polystichum setiferum* (soft shield fern), *Osmunda regalis* (royal fern).

Walls

Adiantum capillus-veneris (maidenhair fern), *Asplenium adiantum-nigrum* (black spleenwort), *Asplenium trichomanes* (maidenhair spleenwort), *Asplenium ruta-muraria* (wall rue), *Athyrium filix-femina* (lady fern), *Ceterach officinarum* (rusty-back fern), *Cystopteris fragilis* (brittle bladder fern), *Phyllitis scolopendrium* (hart's tongue), *Polypodium australe*, *P. interjectum*, *P. vulgare* (common polypody).

Rocky ground

Asplenium adiantum-nigrum (black spleenwort), *Asplenium ruta-muraria* (wall rue), *Asplenium trichomanes* (common maidenhair spleenwort), *Asplenium viride* (green spleenwort), *Dryopteris affinis* (golden-scaled male fern), *Dryopteris filix-mas* (male fern), *Gymnocarpium dryopteris* (oak fern), *Phyllitis scolopendrium* (hart's tongue fern), *Polypodium vulgare* (common polypody), *Polystichum setiferum* (soft shield fern).

Limestone

Adiantum capillus-veneris (maidenhair fern), *Asplenium adiantum-nigrum* (black spleenwort), *Asplenium trichomanes* (common maidenhair spleenwort), *Asplenium viride* (green spleenwort), *Ceterach officinarum* (rusty-back fern), *Cystopteris fragilis* (brittle bladder fern), *Dryopteris submontana* (limestone buckler fern), *Gymnocarpium robertianum* (limestone oak fern), *Phyllitis scolopendrium* (hart's tongue), *Polypodium australe*, *Polystichum aculeatum* (hard shield fern), *Polystichum lonchitis* (holly fern).

Boggy ground

Athyrium filix-femina (lady fern), *Blechnum spicant* (hard fern), *Dryopteris aemula* (hay-scented buckler fern), *Dryopteris carthusiana* (narrow buckler fern), *Dryopteris cristata* (fen buckler fern), *Dryopteris dilatata* (broad buckler fern), *Oreopteris limbosperma* (sweet mountain fern) on damp, peaty uplands, *Osmunda regalis* (royal fern), *Polystichum setiferum* (soft shield fern), *Polystichum aculeatum* (hard shield fern), *Thelypteris palustris* (marsh fern).

Sea cliffs

Adiantum capillus-veneris (maidenhair fern), *Asplenium billotii* (lanceolate spleenwort), *Asplenium marinum* (sea spleenwort).

Mountains

Athyrium distentifolium syn. *A. alpestre* (alpine lady fern), *Cystopteris montana* (mountain bladder fern) (rare), *Dryopteris filix-mas* (male fern), *Dryopteris oreades* (mountain male fern), *Gymnocarpium dryopteris* (oak fern), *Phegopteris connectilis* (beech fern), *Polystichum aculeatum* (hard shield fern) on rocky ledges and in rocky woods, *Polystichum lonchitis* (holly fern) on limestone, *Woodsia ilvensis* (oblong woodsia), *Woodsia alpina* (alpine woodsia).

Scree

Athyrium distentifolium syn *A.* alpestre (alpine lady fern), *Cryptogramma crispa* (parsley fern), *Dryopteris oreades* (mountain buckler fern), *Phegopteris connectilis* (beech fern).

Widespread

Athyrium filix-femina (lady fern), *Dryopteris dilatata* (broad buckler fern), *Dryopteris filix-mas* (male fern), *Phyllitis scolopendrium* (hart's tongue), *Polystichum setiferum* (soft shield fern), *Pteridum aquilinum*.

Rare

Adiantum capillus-veneris (maidenhair fern), *Athyrium distentifolium* syn. *A. alpestre* (alpine lady fern), *A. flexile*, *Asplenium x alternifolium* (alternate-leaved spleenwort), *Asplenium septentrionale* (forked spleenwort), *Cystopteris montana* (mountain bladder fern), *Dryopteris cristata* (fen buckler fern), *Hymenophyllum tunbrigense*, *Hymenophyllum wilsonii* (Wilson's filmy fern),

Trichomanes speciosum (Killarney fern), *Woodsia alpina* (alpine woodsia), *Woodsia ilvensis* (oblong woodsia).

THE FERNS OF NORTH AMERICA

The wide range of climatic conditions prevailing throughout this region, together with a diverse topography, ranging from sun-baked low-lying scrub and swamp-lands to windswept, exposed mountain summits, has helped to sustain the large and varied fern flora of North America.

Habitats

Low-lying swamps and stream banks

The moist, boggy soils in swamps, alongside stream banks and at the open margins of moist woods are the habitats of the largest hardy ferns. Here, *Onoclea sensibilis* (sensitive fern), *Osmunda cinnamomea* (cinnamon fern), *O. Claytoniana* (interrupted fern), *O. regalis* (royal fern) and *Woodwardia virginica* relish the nutrient-rich, sub-acidic soil. With the exception of the latter these ferns have separate fertile leaflets bearing spores in bead-like clusters. Their sterile fronds die back at the onset of frost. The sheltered situation and a constant supply of moisture to their roots allows these long-lived ferns to reach impressive proportions, the fronds of *W. virginica* reaching to 6ft (1.8m).

The margins of swamps and streams is also the habitat of the large evergreen *Dryopteris clintoniana*, *D. cristata*, *Matteuccia pensylvanica* and two *Thelypteris* species, *T. noveboracencis* and *T. palustris*, their fronds ascending in compact erect clusters, reaching, in the case of *D. clintoniana*, to 5ft (1.5m). In northern regions, streamside banks are host to the hardy *Adiantum pedatum*. One of the most resilient *Adiantum*, in moist, sheltered positions *A. pedatum* forms large clumps of almost circular lacy vivid green fronds. Deciduous in open ground, it will remain evergreen in frost-free interiors. The moist rock outcrops alongside fast-flowing rivers in Kentucky and West Virginia provide the constant high humidity necessary for the rare *Trichomanes Boschianum*. This is a challenging species to cultivate, generally requiring the high humidity offered by a closed terrarium.

Swamps and pools throughout this geographic range are host to several aquatic ferns including the two minute species, *Azolla caroliniana*, which extends from New York to Illinois, and *A. mexicana*, widespread from Wisconsin to Bolivia. *Marsilia quadrifolia* (nardoo plant), ranging from Massachusetts to Tennessee, is much larger, less invasive and more suitable for cultivation. *M. quadrifolia*, as its name suggests, has four clover-like leaflets which are held out of the water on half-inch stipes. In cultivation it is suitable for conservatory pools and terrariums.

Woods and forests

The vast areas of deciduous and coniferous woods provide a rich habitat for many North American ferns. In lowland wet woods, the graceful *Athyrium* species, *A. filix-femina* and *A. thelypteroides* (silver fern), together with *Dryopteris austriaca*, the large *D. goldiana* (Goldie's fern) and three *Thelypteris* species, *T. hexagonoptera*, *T. novaboracencis* and *T. simulata* relish the moist, sub-acidic soil and the canopy of shade offered in these habitats.

The cooler thickets and wooded slopes of upland areas offer less humid conditions. Here can be found the more robust ferns which tolerate more open, airy situations and lighter, free-draining soils. These include *Athyrium pycnocarpon* syn *Diplazium pynocarpon*, *Dennstaedtia punctilobula* (hay-scented fern), *Dryopteris filix-mas*, *D. marginalis*, *Gymnocarpium dryopteris* (woodland oak fern), *Polystichum acrostichoides*, *P. braunii* and *Thelypteris phegopteris* (beech fern).

Uplands and mountain slopes

Moist, shady soil banks in upland areas support *Athyrium distentifolium*, *Polypodium polypoides*, *P. vulgare*, *Thelypteris phegopteris* syn. *Phegopteris connectilis* (northern beech fern). With the exception of *Polypodium polypoides* (resurrection fern), these species are also common to North European mountain slopes.

On moist screes and rocky alkaline soils can be found the evergreen *Camptosorus rhizophyllus* (walking fern), which produces plantlets on the tips of its spear-shaped fronds. The free-draining, moist soils of these elevated areas are host to one of the smaller *Dryopteris* species, *D. fragrans*, together with *Gymnocarpium robertianum* (limestone oak fern) and the evergreen *Polystichum lonchitis* (holly fern). In these high exposed positions, inimicable for large, lush-foliaged ferns, the boulder-strewn landscape affords some shelter for the compactly-formed *Cryptogramma* species, *C. Stelleri* and *C. acrostichoides*, together with the *Cystopteris* species, *C. bulbifera*, *C. montana* and *C. fragilis*. Drier screes and rocky terrain offer the arid conditions suitable for four evergreen *Cheilanthes* species. The diminutive *C. Feei*, whose 2–6in. (5–15cm) lacy fronds arise from a compact rhizome, and *C. Alabamensis*, a larger species, its fronds extending 4–12in. (10–30cm) from a slender creeping rhizome, prefer calcareous strata. *C. tormentosa*, fronds 8–18in (20–46cm), and *C. lanosa*, fronds 4–12in (10–30cm), colonize rocks and ledges in subacid soil.

Rock outcrops and gullies

Cliff ledges, ravines and rock outcrops support a rich diversity of fern species. Crannies and fissures afford small and medium-sized ferns shelter from high winds and wide fluctuations of temperature typical in these areas. Amongst moist acidic rocks can be found *Asplenium montanum*, together with the *Woodsia* species, *W. alpina*, *W. ilvensis*, *W. obtusa*, *W. oregana*, and *W. scopulina*. Growing between the crevices of calcareous boulders and on ledges in steep gullies can be found *Asplenium trichomanes*, *A. viride*, *Pellaea atropurpurea*, *Polystichum lonchitis* and the diminutive *Woodsia glabella*. These ferns tolerate some exposure to sun providing their roots are offered cool conditions within sheltered crevices and a constant seepage of moisture. *Adiantum capillus-veneris* can be found in more shaded conditions in these regions, often growing in damp crevices within caves.

Species found in distinct habitats

Swamps

Azolla caroliniana, *Azolla mexicana*, *Dryopteris clintoniana* (Clinton's fern), *Dryopteris cristata* (crested shield fern), *Marsilea quadrifolia* (nardoo plant), *Matteuccia pensylvanica*, *Onoclea sensibilis* (sensitive fern), *Osmunda cinnamomea* (cinnamon fern), *Osmunda Claytoniana* (interrupted fern), *O. regalis* (royal fern), *Selaginella apoda*, *Selaginella selaginoides*, *Thelypteris noveboracencis* (New York fern), *Thelypteris palustris* (marsh fern), *T. simulata*, *Woodwardia areolata* (netted chain fern), *Woodwardia fimbriata* syn. *W. chamissoi* syn. *W. radicans americana*.

Moist woods

Adiantum pedatum, *Athyrium filix-femina* (woodland lady fern), *Athyrium pycnocarpon*, *A. thelypteroides*, *Blechnum spicant* (hard fern), *Botrychium virginianum* (rattlesnake fern), *Campyloneurum phyllitidus* (strap fern), *Cystopteris bulbifera* (bladder fern), *Cystopteris montana*, *Dennstaedtia punctilobula* (hay-scented fern), *Dryopteris arguta*, *Dryopteris austriaca* (spinulose shield fern), *D. clintoniana* (Clinton's fern), *D. cristata* (crested shield fern), *D. expansa* (Northern buckler fern), *D. filix-mas* (common male fern), *D. goldiana* Goldie's fern (giant wood fern), *D. marginalis* (marginal shield fern), *Gymnocarpium dryopteris* (oak fern), *Lygodium palmatum* (Hartford fern/climbing fern), *Onoclea sensibilis* (sensitive fern), *Osmunda Claytoniana* (interrupted fern), *Polypodium polypoides*, *Polypodium scouleri*, *Polystichum acrostichoides* (Christmas fern), *Polystichum braunii*, *Thelypteris hexagonoptera* (broad beech fern), *Thelypteris noveboracencis* (New York fern), *T. phegopteris* (northern beech fern), *T. simulata*, *Woodwardia areolata* (nettled chain fern), *W. fimbriata* syn. *W. chamissoi* syn. *W. radicans americana*, *Woodwardia virginica* (Virginia chain fern).

Upland thickets

Blechnum spicant (hard fern), *Cystopteris fragilis* (brittle bladder fern), *Dryopteris filix-mas* (common male fern), *Dryopteris fragrans*, *D. marginalis* (marginal shield fern), *Gymnocarpium dryopteris* (oak fern), *Polystichum braunii, Polystichum lonchitis* (holly fern), *Woodsia scopulina* subs. *W. s. appalachia.*

Cliff ledges, screes and ravines

Adiantum capillus-veneris, Asplenium montanum, Asplenium trichomanes, A. viride, Athryium distentifolium syn. *A. alpestre, Camptosorus rhizophyllus, Cheilanthes Feei, C. alabamensis, C. lanosa, C. tomentosa, Cryptogramma Stelleri, Cryptogramma acrostichoides, Cystopteris fragilis, Dennstaedtia punctilobula, Dryopteris expansa, Dryopteris fragrans, Gymnocarpium robertianum, Pellaea atropurpurea, Polypodium polypodoides, P. scouleri, P. vulgare, P. lonchitis, P. munitum, Thelypteris phegopteris, Trichomanes Boschianum, Woodsia alpina* syn. *W. hyperborea* (alpine woodsia), *W. glabella, W. ilvensis, W. obtusa, W. oregana* subs. *W. o. cathcartiana, W. scopulina* subs. *W. s. appalachia.*

FERNS OF THE TROPICS

The humid river valleys and mountain forests of the tropics and subtropics are host to the majority of ferns. High rainfall, typically over 84 inches (2 metres) per annum in tropical regions of America, Asia and North Eastern Australia, are coupled with stable temperatures of 75–83°F (24–28°C) throughout the year. Of the 12,000 world-wide fern species, one third are native to tropical America, an area from Southern Florida to Chile. The old world tropics of South East Asia and Malaysia have 4,500 species.

Habitats

Scrub and dry meadows

Although most tropical ferns occur at high altitudes, either in steep ravines, on wet forest floors or epiphytically on tree branches, moss-covered boulders and rocks, a number of genera can be found in scrub, meadow and semi-arid soils. These ferns succeed in exposed, sunny locations, helped by the rugged texture of their fronds which minimize dessication and by lodging their roots into fissures and crevices in the soil, thus exploiting available moisture reservoirs and reducing the roots' exposure to high surface temperatures. These include the species within the genera *Actinopteris, Botrychium, Cheilanthes, Ophioglossum, Pellaea* and *Rumohra*. In cultivation they require a sharp, free-draining soil in open situations. They dislike high humidity and wet conditions.

Lakes and ponds

The tropics of America and Asia are rich in aquatic ferns. The most prolific genus is *Marsilea* with 50 species, 12 of which are native to tropical America. The spores, borne at the base of clover-like leaflets, are adapted to survive long periods, allowing *Marsilea* to exploit seasonally wet areas such as ditches, pools and shallow river courses. The genus *Azolla* contains six species, four native to tropical America. Found floating on the surface of permanent lakes, ponds and quiet rivers, their tiny leaves form large mats of vegetation often completely covering the water. Their common name, mosquito fern, indicates their ability to suppress that insect. *Salvinea*, bearing larger, oval leaflets is a floating aquatic of pantropical distribution. There are ten species, seven of which are native to tropical America. The three species of *Ceratopteris* are the largest aquatic ferns, growing in muddy ditches, lakes, ponds and rivers in the American and Asian tropics. Their fronds, 2–24in (5–61cm), are borne in clusters.

Riverbanks

Along the banks of watercourses, rivers and lakes in tropical regions can be found a wide range of ferns. The moist soil and high humidity of stream banks provide ideal conditions for ferns of lush and soft foliage such as *Adiantum*, the majority of the 200 species being native to the tropics. These habitats are host to the largest fern, *Angiopteris evecta*, a native of Polynesia and Australia, its fronds measuring 7–10ft (2–3m). This species is one of the hundred or so of the Angiopteris genus of pantropical distribution. *Acrostichum*, comprising three species with large spreading fronds of 3–6ft (91cm–1.8m) arising from a stout caudex, is confined to salt-water estuaries and mangrove swamps. The water-washed boulders along streamside banks provide the extremely high humidity necessary for the related genera, *Hymenophyllum* and *Trichomanes*. Although distribution is widespread, the greatest diversity of species occurs in the tropics.

Rocky areas

Many tropical species are adapted to drier, exposed habitats among rocks and boulders. Their compact, leathery fronds are able to withstand exposure to sun and drying winds, allowing them to colonize a variety of open, elevated sites including cliff ledges, rock walls and crevices. Here can be found the genera *Anemia, Anopteris, Asplenium, Coniogramme, Dennstaedtia, Doryopteris, Gymnopteris, Hemionitis, Paesia, Pityrogramma* and *Pteris*.

Ravines

Steep ravines, flushed by mineral-rich streams, provide a varied habitat for a diverse range of ferns. On damp rocks in light shade grow small ferns such as *Anemia*, *Anogramma* and *Asplenium*. In deeper shade at the base of ravines, in pockets of fertile soil washed down from mountain slopes by heavy rains, can be found the tree ferns, *Alsophila*, *Cibotium*, *Cyathea* and *Dicksonia*.

Forest

Wet mountain forests, reaching to 6,000 feet, are host to the majority of the ferns of this climatic region. Deep shade and moist, mainly acidic soils create ideal conditions for many of the largest ferns, including the tree ferns, such as *Cibotium*, *Ctenitis*, *Cyathea*, and *Dicksonia*. Here also can be found many species of *Athyrium*, *Blechnum*, *Denstaedtia* and *Dryopteris*. In the warm, humid conditions of the tropics these ferns are larger and more luxuriant than examples of the genera found in the temperate zones.

Epiphytes

With a high density of ground vegetation in tropical forests and the intense competition for terrestial sites, many fern species have adapted to growing epiphytically on trees, rotting logs and mossy boulders. *Nephrolepsis*, *Davallia*, *Platycerium* and *Polypodium* – the most familiar indoor ferns – belong to this group.

Genera found in distinct habitats

Scrub and dry meadows

Actinopteris, Botrichium, Cheilanthes, Ophioglossum, Pellaea, Rumohra.

Lakes and ponds

Azolla, Ceratopteris, Marsilea, Salvinia.

Riverbanks

Acrostichum, Adiantum, Alsophila, Ampelopteris, Angiopteris, Anogramma, Ctenitis, Didymochlaena, Equisetum, Hemionitis, Hymenophyllum, Lastreopsis, Leptopteris, Marattia, Microgramma, Tectaria, Trichomanes.

Rocky areas

Anopteris, Asplenium, Coniogramme, Dennstaedtia, Doryopteris, Gymnopteris, Hemionitis, Paesia, Pityrogramma, Pteris.

Ravines

Alsophila, Anemia, Anogramma, Anopteris, Arachniodes, Asplenium, Cibotium,

Ctenitis, Cyathea, Cyrtomium, Dicksonia, Diplazium, Dryopteris, Lastreopsis, Marattia, Microlepia.

Forests

Athyrium, Blechnum, Cibotium, Ctenitis, Culcita, Denstaedtia, Dryopteris, Lindsaya, Macrothelypteris.

Epiphytes

Aglaomorpha, Belvisia, Camplyoneurum, Davallia, Dictymia, Drymoglossum, Drynaria, Elaphoglossum, Humata, Lemmaphyllum, Lygodium, Nephrolepis, Oleandra, Phlebodium, Platycerium, Pleopeltis, Polypodium, Pyrrosia, Scyphularia, Selliguea, Stenochlaena, Vittaria.

4

PREPARATION FOR FERN CULTIVATION OUTDOORS

Ferns give to any garden, throughout the changing seasons, an unrivalled diversity of colour and form. The vivid green tints of the unfurling fronds usher in the spring with intense freshness and, later in the year, those same fronds tinged with a myriad of russet hues signal the onset of winter.

One of the most pleasing attributes of ferns is their ability to prosper in conditions where sun-loving plants would quickly die. A remarkably easy group of plants to cultivate, they require only the minimum of site preparation – allowing even new gardens or poorly maintained sites to be adapted quickly to successful fern growing.

Evaluating sites

In any planting scheme a little time spent in planning will be richly rewarded with healthy, vigorous specimens. The main requirement of all ferns is the provision of an adequate supply of moisture throughout the growing period. If soil conditions are unsuitable, ferns can soon wilt beyond recovery during the driest periods of summer. However, good preparation of the planting site – whether it be in open ground or container – will ensure that ferns will get through all but the driest periods without recourse to frequent additional watering. The two most important elements in ensuring that moisture is available to the growing ferns are correct soil composition, and adequate provision of shade.

Soil composition

While most ferns for garden cultivation will prefer a humus-rich, free-draining soil, it is quite possible to find ferns that will prosper in the most extreme types of garden soil. By exploiting the prevailing soil conditions, most gardens will be capable of sustaining a range of ferns without recourse to the expense and labour of restructuring the existing soil. However, rather than proceeding by trial and error, incurring disappointments on the way, it will be more practical to determine the state of the soil and match it with fern species which are known to prosper in these conditions. To maximize success, it will be useful to determine whether the soil is acidic, neutral or alkaline. A pH testing kit is a simple and accurate method of matching fern species to existing soil conditions. Generally, a neutral to slightly acid soil, pH 7–6.5, will suit the majority of ferns. Ferns whose natural habitats are among the crannies and fissures of rocks and scree will prefer an alkaline soil, pH 7.5–8.0.

The texture and composition of existing garden soil should be carefully scrutinized. Garden soil is composed of a mixture of inorganic particles – clays, gravels and sands – and organic matter – humus – originating from decayed plant material. This is the basic skeleton of the soil and the proportions of each of the elements present in the soil will determine its crumb structure. A soil with a good crumb structure will contain approximately 50 per cent sand, 30 per cent gravel and 20 per cent clay. This type of soil can suspend good volumes of air, and water. The humus present in the soil binds together the crumbs and provides materials for earthworms to further aerate the soil and for the soil bacteria to produce plant foods.

Acid soils

A soil which has a high proportion of clay, 30 per cent plus, is poorly aerated and difficult to cultivate. It is prone to waterlogging in wet weather and caking in dry periods. Slow to warm up in spring, its composition tends to create stagnant, airless conditions which retard and restrict root growth. Although it contains large amounts of plant foods, it is in its most extreme form inhospitable for most plants. Unadapted, most clay soils can support some of the more tolerant woodland species such as the *Athyrium*, *Blechnum*, *Dryopteris* and *Thelypteris* species, even though they do not provide ideal conditions. The addition of coarse grit or small stones forked into the soil where the ferns are to be planted will assist in improving aeration and drainage around the fern roots.

Spongy, peaty soils can be strongly acidic. Generally waterlogged, the large amounts of organic matter present are not sufficiently decomposed to be accessible to plants. Here *Acrostichum* and *Blechnum* species together with wetland ferns such as *Gymnocarpium dryopteris*, *Thelypteris* species, *Onoclea sensibilis* and *Osmunda* species would be sufficiently compatible with prevailing conditions. Again, the addition of grit or small stones to the soil around the plants will improve drainage.

Sandy soils are deficient in clay and impoverished in plant foods. The porous nature of these soils contributes to the leaching of nutrients, and tends to create acidic conditions. However, good aeration of plant roots and the ability to warm up quickly in the spring makes this soil viable for many species, although the dryness of the soil in the peak summer months will entail additional watering. The ferns of arid regions are a good choice for this soil. These ferns can tolerate high surface temperatures and drought if their roots are sufficiently sheltered within the crevices and crannies of their native habitats. *Actinopteris*, *Cheilanthes*, *Cryptogramma*, *Pellaea* and *Pteris* will tolerate dry conditions.

Alkaline soils

Chalk soils are shallow and deficient in plant nutrients. Drying out quickly in summer, they do not allow sufficient moisture retention around the roots, essential for most ferns. In this type of soil a natural choice would be those ferns native to shallow limestone soils, such as many of the *Asplenium* species, *Cystopteris*, *Dryopteris*, *Pellaea* and *Polystichum*.

Neutral soils

Loams are the ideal garden soils. Their crumbly texture makes them easy to work and, if they contain plenty of organic material, they offer an optimum growing medium for the majority of fern species.

An alternative to open planting in those gardens with difficult soil is to use pot-grown ferns in the garden. This type of cultivation is most suitable for medium-sized ferns with erect or ascending rootstock. The pot should be plunged into the soil up to its rim. Although these pot-grown plants will require more frequent watering and feeding than plants grown in open ground, they can provide a valuable display in new or neglected gardens for an interim period prior to making improvements to the soil.

Restructuring the soil

In the small or medium-sized garden some consideration might be given to restructuring the existing soil. The benefits in terms of increasing the range of fern cultivation and reducing the burden of maintenance in subsequent years far outweigh the labours incurred.

The drainage of clay soils can be improved by the addition of a liberal quantity of well-rotted leafmould, peat and coarse grit or gravel in equal proportions by volume. This will increase the aeration of the soil around the plant roots. Garden lime (3oz per sq. yd) applied to the dry soils in autumn will improve the crumb structure. Some slight increase in alkalinity of the soil can be expected as a result of adding lime. As the structure of clay soils is easily damaged, care will need to be taken when working these soils. They should only be worked on when dry. Avoid digging or walking on these soils when they are wet, for the inevitable compaction of the ground will destroy its texture and form it into puddled clay, making it subsequently impervious to water and air.

Moisture-retentiveness in dry soils can be increased by the addition of organic material such as humus, peat or leafmould. Leafmould is the most suitable material in terms of cost and availability. It is best to store freshly gathered leaves in mesh cages open to the weather during winter. In spring, the partially decomposed leaves should be forked into the ground. Alternatively, where the garden has yet to be cultivated, and there is no risk to plants of any fungal disease being harboured in the mulch, the leafmould can be applied directly to the ground in autumn. The action of worms will draw down into the soil the nutrient-rich leafmould. In spring, before planting, ensure any remaining leaves are forked into the soil.

Adapting sites to suit more difficult subjects

Where the garden soil is strongly acid or alkaline there will be little point in altering its pH value to cater for particularly desired species of ferns. Over a short period of time the soil will revert to its original state. A longer-term solution would be to consruct areas of raised beds.

In gardens where the soil is acid, raised beds of alkaline soil can be made from the basic soil with the addition of lime. Generally, a looser-textured planting medium is required for alkaline-preferring species. The bed should be well drained, with a layer of broken brick or rubble 6in. (15cm) in depth covering the original soil level. Fill in the bed with the excavated soil together with a liberal quantity of leafmould. To achieve the necessary alkalinity and open texture, limestone chippings and small stones should be added to the soil. The perimeter of the bed can be made from a variety of materials such as cut logs, brickwork or rockwork. The latter is preferable, especially if limestone rocks are available. To provide some interest in the sides of the bed, small, alkaline-preferring fern species can be planted in the crevices between the rocks.

Acid beds in alkaline gardens can be constructed on the same principle. Here, soil from the garden should not be used. The soil mix should be composed of one part each of acid loam, peat and lime-free gravel to two parts leafmould. The bed should be sufficiently deep, at least 18in. (46cm), to keep the ferns' roots out of contact with the alkaline soil below. Cut logs, acid rocks or brickwork will be suitable for the perimeter. A wall of peat blocks can produce a pleasing effect, particularly where small ferns of acid habitats are planted between the blocks.

Providing shade

Some species, such as *Asplenium trichomanes* (maidenhair spleenwort), *Ceterach officinarum* (rusty-back fern), *Cheilanthes*, *Dryopteris filix-mas* (male fern), and *Pellaea* species will withstand constant exposure to full sunlight throughout the day. However, the ideal site for most ferns, and particularly the more delicate and finely-formed species, will offer a degree of shade during some part of the day. Not only will this help the ferns to recover from the inevitable drying out of the soil around the plants, and subsequent wilting of the fronds, but it will serve also to heighten the colour saturation of their display.

A valuable preparation for fern cultivation would involve making a shade map of the garden. This would consist of sketching on paper, at hourly intervals, that part of the garden which is currently in shade. Clearly, there is no need to complete this at one sitting: a series of observations over a fortnight or so, taken at different hours of the day, will provide a good basis for an evaluation of suitable planting sites which can offer an adequate degree of shade to your ferns.

A wall, of either stone or brick, is a valuable asset in the fern garden. It not only offers the garden the benefit of shade for part of the day, but also provides a natural planting area in the mortar for the smaller ferns such as *Asplenium* species, *Ceterach officinarum* (rusty-back fern), *Cheilanthes, Phyllitis scolopendrium* (hart's tongue fern), *Polypodium* and *Woodsia* species.

Other forms of shading, offered by fences and the overhanging branches of trees, can be useful in providing shelter for the larger fern species associated with woodlands and hedgebanks, such as *Athyrium, Dryopteris, Gymnocarpium dryopteris* and *Woodwardia* species. With more finely-formed ferns, such as *Adiantum* and most evergreen species, the drip of water droplets from branches may prove injurious to their fronds. Honeydew secretions, dropping down from the leaves onto fronds, may also be a source of fungal diseases in evergreen ferns in this situation. For these reasons more robust, deciduous forms will prove to be the best choice for under trees.

Exploiting the garden's microclimate

Even the smallest garden will contain variations of temperature, humidity and rainfall. These slight variations can be exploited to maximize success in fern cultivation. Careful siting of species can ameliorate some of the more punitive effects of prevailing climatic conditions.

Winds can not only damage the fronds of ferns, but can cause severe deterioration of the plant by drying the soil around the roots. Damage can be minimized by providing open-textured wind-breaks such as hedges and slatted fencing which will lessen the intensity of winds. Solid wind-breaks will funnel the air, intensifying the turbulence on the leeward side around the plant, exacerbating the damage.

The influence of exterior walls and fences on the microclimate of the garden can be utilized in choosing fern sites. Borders sited against south-facing walls will generally be too dry for many fern species, but may be useful for more tender, xerophytic species which have been introduced into wet climates. Here, the wall will reduce rainfall on the soil and the sun's heat will be radiated from the wall onto the nearby plants. North-facing walls will prove more suitable for tender ferns of moist habitats, where some loss of available rainfall is offset against the benefit of less extreme fluctuations in day and night temperatures. Protection from extremes of temperature can be found in other parts of the garden by exploiting the envelopes of stable air underneath shrubs and trees.

Where semi-tender species are grown outdoors in frost-prone climates, raised areas of the garden should be chosen as sites. These areas will offer more frost protection than low-lying parts of the garden where colder air will collect to form frost-pockets. Further protection can be given to frost-tender species by covering the plants during cold, wet periods with glass or plastic cloches.

In areas of low rainfall, evaporation of moisture from the soil around the roots of ferns can be minimized by exploiting the shade cast by small boulders and rocks. A mulch of bark, peat or gravel will also mitigate dessication of the soil.

Planting ferns

Planting out can be undertaken at any time between mid spring and early autumn. Plants which are obtained in the winter months should be plunged in a peat-based medium where the roots can be kept moist and sheltered until spring. Pot-grown specimens obtained from garden centres and nurseries should be inspected carefully to ensure that the soil has not dried out. If the soil has been allowed to dry, the plants should be discarded.

Soak newly-obtained plants overnight before removing from the original pot. The roots should be carefully teased from the soil and replanted in a prepared bed. Plant clump-forming rootstock to a depth where the crown is just above the soil level. Plants with creeping rhizomes should be planted with the rhizomes an inch below the soil. Newly obtained plants will benefit by being placed in a nursery bed for the first season where a check can be more easily made on their progress. In the first year it is advisable to provide additional watering while the plant developes a good root system. If planted in congenial sites which offer shade during the hottest part of the day, many mature ferns will not require additional watering except during particularly dry periods.

Seasonal care

In spring, before the new fronds emerge, carefully cut back the previous year's fronds and then clear any remnants of mulch that have not fully rotted down. Remove any debris around the plants that may harbour pests and fungal diseases. Slugs may prove the most persistent enemy of young ferns, particularly *Adiantum* and *Asplenium*. Traps or bait are effective weapons against these creatures who will thrive in the damp, shady fern garden.

In late spring and summer, when plants are growing vigorously, some additional watering will be needed for young ferns and those ferns in more exposed situations. There can be no hard-and-fast prescription offered for watering routines in open ground. Too much watering can be as detrimental as too little, and often more so. The moisture needs of particular species, the composition of the soil, the garden's exposure to sun and drying winds, together with the possible presence of large shrubs will determine the need for supplementary watering. The careful and vigilant gardener will quickly discover the risk areas in the garden, where the soil is prone to dryness. When a need for watering is indicated, a thorough soaking of the ground to a depth of six inches should be given.

In autumn, a mulch of well-rotted leafmould, peat or bark chippings should be given to ferns planted in open sites. Generally, ferns will need no additional feeding if soil conditions are good. Should ferns show signs of nutrient deficiency, such as slow growth or yellowing of the growing fronds, apply a dressing of slow-release fertilizer such as bonemeal or fishmeal at half the recommended strength in spring and summer.

In winter the fronds of deciduous ferns can be cut back to an inch above the crown. In areas subject to frost, the decayed fronds will provide some protection to the plant and should not be removed until the spring growth of new fronds shows signs of emerging.

Ferns for temperate regions

In temperate regions hardy species will form the core of fern planting. However, with some forethought many semi-hardy and tender species can be chosen for the temperate garden, if some protection indoors can be offered during the coldest months. These non-hardy species can be grown in pots plunged into the soil, or alternatively, they can be used in rafts and baskets attached to or suspended from fencing or branches.

Ferns in subtropical climates

With the exception of the ferns of arid habitats, which are able to withstand high temperatures if their roots are sheltered, some degree of shade should be offered to ferns growing in open ground. Where the garden has a particularly open aspect with little natural shade, some thought could be given to constructing a lath house.

Lath houses, constructed on greenhouse principles using wooden slats, generally six inches wide with a similar-sized gap between each, are ideal structures within which to grow ferns, offering protection from the sun and drying winds. Such structures allow an optimum balance of light, shade, ventilation and humidity necessary to those ferns whose natural habitats are the moist, shady tropical and subtropical woodlands and forests.

In areas of low rainfall, some form of permanent irrigation will be needed in the garden. Plastic pipes, perforated at intervals along their length, may either be buried below the surface or located along the edges of borders. After the initial labour of installation such a system allows the gardener the luxury of semi-automatic watering throughout the seasons.

Ferns require a period of dormancy, usually during the winter months. The additional watering given during spring and summer should be reduced in autumn. In winter, potted outdoor ferns should be kept barely moist. In warm regions hardy, deciduous species may remain evergreen. If kept over-moist new, stunted fronds will continue to emerge, dissipating the plant's vigour. Remove such new growths as they appear and try to ensure that the soil around the plant does not remain too moist at this time.

Pests and diseases of ferns

Ferns offered good growing conditions are rarely troubled by pests and diseases. Good housekeeping – removing plant debris and periodic checking of plants for any signs of trouble – will minimize damage to stocks.

In outdoor areas devoted entirely to ferns, slugs will be the major enemy, especially in spring when emerging fronds will be prey to attack. *Adiantum* species are particularly vulnerable. Slug bait is an effective deterrent, though this treatment is not advisable where children or pets use the garden. The great Victorian fern gardener E.J. Lowe, in his book *Fern Growing* (1891), advocated the use of slug traps composed of dishes containing a mash of beer and bran. Set down between the ferns at dusk, they were inspected during the hours of darkness and the offending creatures caught whilst feeding on the mixture. Lowe recalls trapping several hundred in one night.

Where ferns are grown alongside other garden plants additional, less-injurious infestations can be expected to be transmitted to the ferns.

Aphids, mealy bugs, thrips and scale insects may transfer onto fern fronds from other plants. These infestations are best dealt with by daily spraying of a weak solution of liquid detergent. Where infestations are significantly high, it may be advisable to treat the surrounding plants with a proprietary insecticide. The use of insecticide is not advisable on ferns except in very dilute form. It is far better to remove and burn heavily infested fronds.

5
GROWING FERNS IN SMALL GARDENS

FERNS FOR PATIOS AND COURTYARDS

Whether your garden is the postage-stamp size patio of a town house or the enclosed yard of a terrace, ferns can do much to enhance these small, often shaded areas. In temperate climates, where frost will destroy non-hardy plants, the availability of a heated area indoors will allow the many interesting semi-hardy, semi-tender and tender species of fern to be included in outdoor planting schemes. In autumn these non-hardy species can be brought indoors, until the danger of frost is passed in the following late spring. Tender species of the tropics will require minimum winter temperatures of 60°F (15°C), whilst semi-tender species require minimum winter temperatures of 50°F (10°C). Semi-hardy species can be over-wintered under cover in unheated areas, but will appreciate a minimum temperature of 40°F (5°C).

These small planting areas are more sheltered from the weather than the larger expanses of open gardens. The warmth emanating from the house, together with the shelter created by walls and fencing, tend to make a courtyard or patio rather drier than the prevailing climatic factors might otherwise indicate, and therefore more care will need to be taken to protect ferns from over-arid conditions and to ensure that they can receive an adequate supply of moisture. This is particularly important where ferns are grown in pots, baskets or other containers.

Soil mixes

Ferns planted in beds and borders within small, enclosed areas will need plenty of moisture-retentive humus to compensate for the effects of reduced humidity and rainfall. By far the best, and most widely available form of humus is leafmould. This will hold moisture better than peat, and over time will decompose to generate plant nutrients. Furthermore, leafmould will encourage the activity of earthworms, thereby aerating the soil and increasing its moisture-retentive capacity. Although leafmould should be overwintered to decompose before application to the soil, it is generally not practical to store sufficient quantities in the limited space available to the courtyard gardener. In these circumstances, the leafmould should be forked in with the existing soil to a depth of 6–8 inches. A balance, by volume, of 50 per cent leafmould and soil will not be too much. In clay soil, where initial aeration will be poor, a generous application of coarse, horticultural-grade sand or lime-free grit, along with the added humus, will help to improve the soil.

CREATING A SMALL FERNERY

The fernery was a Victorian innovation which allowed the fern enthusiast to indulge in his pursuit regardless of the scale of his garden. Commonly, these ferneries incorporated another Victorian gardening innovation, the rockery, in their layout. Often featuring ornate grottoes and fairy dells, they reflected the industry and obsessive care that the Victorian gardener devoted to seeking to mirror, or re-interpret, in miniature, the natural world.

The type of rocks incorporated in the fernery will, in part, determine the pH of the soil and therefore the selection of species. To create alkaline conditions limestone rocks should be used in the construction. Where this is impractical, ground lime should be added to the soil. If the latter method is used, the leaching of lime from the soil will have to be compensated by periodic replenishment. A neutral-to-acid soil can be created by using granite rock or slate in place of limestone rock.

In the small garden, however, rockwork can look incongruous unless a high degree of skill, of hand and eye, is employed in its design. A natural appearance should be the effect sought, both in the structure of the site and in the species growing in it. Imitating natural, indigenous geological formations and exploiting local rocks will add authenticity to the rockery, regardless of its scale. Similarly, in the choosing of species it should be borne in mind that native ferns which are of rocky habitats, will create a more harmonious effect than non-native species.

An alternative site for a fernery would be a sloping, shaded part of the garden. Here the acid-loving ferns of the hedgerow and woodland could inspire the choice of fern species. The soil should be deeply dug and supplemented with plenty of leafmould and coarse grit.

The prevailing climate will determine whether semi-tender and tender ferns can be planted directly into the soil. Where species are likely to suffer frost damage, potted specimens may remain in their pots and be plunged into larger containers lined with peat, or planted in open ground during late spring when the risk of frost has gone. Bury the pot up to its brim in the plunge material, and ensure that both the individual pots and the container are well watered. It is important to be especially vigilant in looking after the moisture requirements of such temporary plantings. There is the danger that the soil within the pot will become over-dry even when the surrounding soil is still moist.

The particularly fine varietal forms which have been collected from the wild or hybridized by enthusiasts should be high on the list for inclusion in the fernery. When planting the ferns ensure that there is enough room between the plants to allow the fronds to spread unhindered. A spacing of three feet between young ferns of the *Athyrium*, *Dryopteris*, and *Polystichum* genera is desirable, with a lesser amount usually being adequate for the small forms of *Adiantum*, *Asplenium*, *Pellaea* and *Phyllitis scolopendrium*. After the ferns have developed over a number of years they may need to be re-spaced, in early spring, to take account of their increasing size. Be sure to leave the roots as undisturbed as possible when removing and replanting, and give more attention to watering in the following months.

Ferns for a small fernery

Small ferns up to 12in. (30cm)

The mark ★ indicates that the plant is hardy and will withstand cultivation in open ground in climates where winter temperatures may be expected to reach 22°F (−5°C) minimum.

Acid/neutral soils

Adiantum spp., *Adiantum pedatum* vars.★, *Anemia adiantifolia*, *A. rotundifolia*, *A. phyllitidis*, *Anogramma chaerophylla*, *Athyrium filix-femina* vars.★, *Blechnum penna-marina*, *B. spicant*★, *Cryptogramma acrostichoides*, *C. crispa*★, *C. stelleri*, *Doryopteris concolor*, *D. ludens*, *D. pedata*, *D. oreades*★, *Gymnocarpium dryopteris*★, *Phyllitis scolopendrium crispum*★, *Polypodium* spp., *Polypodium vulgare*★, *Polystichum setiferum* vars.★, *Pteris cretica*, *P. ensiforma*, *Thelypteris phegopteris*★, *Woodsia alpina*★, *W. ilvensis*★, *W. scopulina*★.

Alkaline soils

Actinopteris australis, *Adiantum capillus-veneris*, *Anogramma chaerophylia*, *Asplenium adiantum-nigrum*★, *A. trichomanes*★, *Camptosorus rhizophyllus*, *Ceterach aureum*, *C. officinarum*★, *C. dalhousiae*, *Cheilanthes alabamensis*, *C. feii*, *C. fragrans*, *C. pulchella*, *Cystopteris alpina*★, *C. dickieana*★, *C. bulbifera*, *C. fragilis*★, *C. montana*★, *Cyrtomium falcatum*, *Gymnocarpium robertianum*★, *Phyllitis scolopendrium crispum*★, *Polystichum* spp.★, *Woodsia glabella*★.

FERNS IN CONTAINERS

The pot-grown fern represents a compromise in cultivation. Combining aesthetics with convenience, pots can be moved and removed to suit both the decorative fancy of the gardener and the vagaries of the climate. Such pleasing practicality must be balanced against the potential detriment to plants that this form of cultivation entails. It is often overlooked that pot-grown plants are more vulnerable to waterlogging and drought than those grown in the open garden.

Ferns grown in pots and other containers will need a moisture-retentive, fertile soil. Garden soil, often insufficiently fertile and harbouring potential plant pests, may not prove a satisfactory substitute for those soilless composts specifically designed for container-grown plants. Commercial soilless mixes, generally incorporating a 50 per cent mixture of moss peat or other organic material and coarse sand, together with trace mineral and fertilizers, are suitable for a broad range of container-grown ferns. Even with these balanced composts the addition of a well-rotted leafmould will further improve moisture retentiveness and provide a more long-lasting nutrient supply. Where leafmould is added, it should make up one quarter by volume of the planting mix.

For ferns with more specific soil preferences such compost can be modified easily to fulfil requirements. For alkaline-preferring species additional limestone should be added to the basic compost. This can be in the form of ground limestone, one ounce per cubic foot of compost, or limestone chippings. To ensure a correct balance the mix should be checked to ensure the pH is in the range 7–8. For those ferns, such as the epiphytic species, which require particularly good drainage, coarse grit should be added to the basic compost. Ferns of woodland habitats, which prefer a more moist, strongly acidic compost, with a pH of 5.5–6.5, will need additional peat or well-rotted leafmould, up to 50 per cent by volume, added to the compost. Again, soil testing will determine whether sufficient levels of acidity have been reached.

Plants must be matched to compatible soil conditions and size of pot. Even with good initial soil conditions pot-grown plants will certainly fail to make good growth, and may quickly expire, if planted in an unsuitable size of pot. Under-potted ferns, where plants have outgrown their containers, exhibit poor, stunted growth and require frequent watering. Their young fronds will be rather yellowed in appearance. Such root-bound plants should be removed from their pots as soon as this is practicable. Any remaining old compost can be shaken from the roots and, to stimulate new root-growth, the old, matted roots should be carefully teased out. For pot-bound plants, choose a pot one size up from the previous one. Broken pieces of brick or crocks over the drain hole will assist drainage and help prevent the plant becoming waterlogged. Small pots, up to six inches, need a one or two-inch layer of drainage. Larger pots may require up to four inches of drainage material.

Both clay and plastic pots are suitable for fern cultivation. For larger ferns, clay pots are to be preferred. More pleasing in appearance than plastic pots, their weight makes them less likely to keel over in strong winds. However, in unglazed pots the soil will dry more quickly, and thus require more vigilance in watering. With smaller ferns, and particularly when there are many young plants needing frequent repotting, plastic pots are more practicable. These will involve the gardener in marginally less-frequent watering than the clay varieties, and they will stand more careless handling than fragile clay pots will allow.

Avoid the temptation to over-pot. Ferns which are over-potted are unable to take up the available moisture present in the soil since their roots cannot reach it. The soil becomes waterlogged and sour, preventing air reaching the plant roots. Growth will be stunted, fronds yellowed and the plant vulnerable to fungal disease. As a general rule, a correct-sized pot should be just sufficient to contain the fern's roots. Ferns with ascending or erect rootstock, the most suitable type for pot cultivation, should be planted with their crowns just above the level of the soil. A gap of half to one inch should be left between the top of the soil and the rim of the pot to allow for watering. After planting, water the soil thoroughly, and allow the surplus water to drain from the pot. Do not water again until the soil shows signs of becoming dry. The aim in watering container-grown plants is to give the plant a good soaking and allow the soil to become almost dry before watering again. Topping up with small amounts of water, at frequent intervals, has the effect of choking the plant's roots. The practice of standing plants in saucers of water is also to be avoided, as this results in permanent waterlogging of the plant. Inevitably, such misguided kindness, if uncorrected, will result in the loss of the plant.

In temperate regions, temporary planting should be brought in in early autumn to over-winter in suitably sheltered areas indoors. In either outdoor or indoor areas, the ferns will require little additional watering during their dormant period. In either situation the soil should be kept barely moist. Resume additional watering in early spring when the emergence of new growth will indicate the end of dormancy. Old fronds, which may be kept on deciduous over-wintering ferns to give some frost protection, should be removed at this time.

Newly potted ferns will not need additional feeding. A good compost, containing an equal mix of commercial compost and well-rotted leafmould, will last most ferns until they are repotted. Ferns in their final pot should be fed with a slow-release organic fertilizer at half the recommended strength during spring and summer. Alternatively, in spring, remove the top layer of soil to a depth of two or three inches and replace it with fresh compost. Ensure a regular watering regime for ferns grown in pots and containers. For most ferns, a moist but not soggy soil represents the conditions closest to those found in their native habitats. To ensure these conditions most pots and containers will need to be watered at least once a week from spring to autumn. Where plants are in exposed positions, watering may be required twice a week. Watering routines should take account of prevailing weather conditions. In very wet periods suspend hand watering to avoid keeping the ferns in a waterlogged soil. In periods of prolonged dry weather plants may need to be watered every evening.

Tubs and troughs can be particularly good sites for many species of ferns and, when placed close to a patio door or a window, will allow close observation of the ferns' interesting and varied foliage. In these locations, where delicacy of form can be most readily appreciated, dwarf and low-growing forms might be chosen. The standard fern-potting compost mixture should be used for those ferns which do not require an alkaline soil. For those ferns which require an alkaline soil, a quantity of ground limestone or limestone chipping should be added to the standard compost.

The containers need to have drainage holes to allow surplus water to escape and to prevent the soil becoming waterlogged. Plastic containers without drainage can be drilled or pierced with an old screwdriver that has been heated over a gas flame. Fill the container to one quarter of its volume with broken bricks or small stones to ensure adequate drainage. Make up the remainder of the container with fern compost, leaving at least one inch between the top of the soil and the rim of the container. This will allow rainwater to collect and minimize hand watering in the future.

The container should be well watered after planting, but resist the temptation to over-water in the following weeks – as many ferns die through over-watering as through drought. If the container is sited out of direct sun and is not over-planted with ferns, the plants should thrive without much additional hand watering.

Ferns for pots and containers
(* indicates hardy fern, *see* p. 51)

Ferns to 12in.(30cm)

Acid soils

Adiantum spp., *Adiantum pedatum* vars.*, *Anemia adiantifolia*, *A. phyllitidis*, *A. rotundifolia*, *Anogramma chaerophylla*, *Athyrium filix-femina**, *Blechnum penna-marina*, *B. spicant**, *Cryptogramma acrostichoides*, *C. crispa**, *C. Stelleri*, *Doryopteris concolor*, *D. ludens*, *D. pedata*, *Dryopteris affinis crispa congesta**, *Gymnocarpium dryopteris**, *Phyllitis scolopendrium* vars.*, *Polypodium* spp., *Polypodium vulgare**, *Pteris cretica*, *P. ensiforma*, *Thelypteris phegopteris**, *Woodsia alpina**, *W. ilvensis**, *W. scopulina**.

Alkaline soils

Actinopteris australis, *Adiantum capillus-veneris*, *Anogramma chaerophylla*, *Asplenium adiantum-nigrum*, *A. trichomanes**, *Camptosorus rhizophyllus*, *Ceterach aureum*, *C. officinarum**, *C. dalhousiae*, *Cheilanthes alabamensis*, *C. Feii*, *C. fragrans*, *C. pulchella*, *Cystopteris alpina**, *C. dickieana**, *C. bulbifera*, *C.*

fragilis★, *C. montana*★. *Cyrtomium falcatum*, *Gymnocarpium robertianum*★, *Phyllitis scolopendrium* vars.★. *Polystichum* spp.★, *Woodsia glabella*★.

Ferns 12–36in. (30–90cm)

Acid soils

Adiantum hispidulum, *A. pedatum* vars.★, *Anemia adiantifolia*, *A. phyllitidis*, *Asplenium bulbiferum*, *A. daucifolium*, *Blechnum auriculatum*, *B. spicant*★, *Dennstaedtia punctilobula*★, *Dryopteris* spp.★, *Matteuccia struthiopteris*★, *Pityrogramma* spp, *Polypodium* spp., *Polystichum aculeatum*★, *P. scouleri*★, *P. acrostichoides*★, *Pteris* spp., *Thelypteris hexagonoptera*★, *T. novaboracensis*★, *T. phegopteris*★, *Thelypteris* spp.

Alkaline soils

Cyrtomium falcatum, *Cystopteris bulbifera*, *Gymnocarpium robertianum*★, *Pellaea atropurpurea*★, *Pellaea* spp., *Phyllitis scolopendrium* vars.★, *Polystichum* spp.★.

BASKETS AND RAFTS

While ferns with ascending rootstock or crowns, throwing up their fronds in erect shuttlecocks, such as *Athyrium* and *Dryopteris*, are displayed to advantage in pots, those ferns with short, creeping rhizomes such as *Davallia* or *Polypodium* are often more suited to basket or raft cultivation. The drooping habit of the fronds of ferns with creeping rhizomes are especially suited to this form of cultivation, where an elevated position will allow a more interesting vantage point from which to view their cascading beauty. Even when the ferns are dormant and bereft of fronds, the delightful texture and geometry of the rhizomes emerging through the circle of moss, or in maturity, growing over the moss, makes this type of planting well worth undertaking.

Suspended from beams, or by brackets attached to stonework or trellising, baskets can add a new dimension to small gardens. In temperate climates hardy varieties may be left in position, provided that they are not exposed to wind damage. Where winter frosts can be expected, baskets planted with semi–tender and tender species will need to be brought indoors in autumn and given the protection of minimum temperatures of 50°F (10°C) and 60°F (16°C) respectively.

Potted ferns will need to be prepared for basket display by removing them from pots and gently teasing the rhizomes from the soil ball. With larger plants it may be more practical to wash the soil from the rhizomes before arranging them in the basket.

Line the basket or wooden raft with layers of moss, to a depth of two to three inches. Arrange the fern in the centre of the container with the rhizomes spread around the inner circumference and the crown just below the level of the container. Fill the container to three-quarters its volume with an open-textured compost, composed of one part, by volume, of gravel, soilless compost and rotted leafmould. Complete the planting by placing a layer of moss over the potting mix. Ensure that the vertical growing tip is not covered with soil or moss.

Feeding and watering of baskets and rafts

Initial and subsequent watering is best achieved by immersing the basket in a basin of water for 15 minutes until well soaked. Hang the basket in a suitable spot to drain the surplus water before returning it to its chosen site. The condition of the sphagnum moss lining will give some indication of the need to water the basket or raft. A yellowing of the moss will indicate that watering is required. If the moss is a deep green colour the container has adequate moisture. Baskets and rafts should not be replanted annually. Most plantings will take two years to achieve their most interesting state, where the rhizomes emerge through the mossy circumference, creating a ball of frond foliage. A slow-release organic fertilizer such as fishmeal should be applied at half the recommended strength to the soil each spring. If young growth shows signs of nutrient deficiency fertilize the soil again in summer. In late autumn reduce the frequency of watering, but do not allow the container to become dry. In temperate climates, semi-tender and tender basket ferns should be brought indoors where they should be kept barely moist throughout the winter. Some loss of fronds can be expected when the ferns enter their dormant period. In early spring new growth will re-emerge. When growth recommences apply an organic fertilizer and water the container thoroughly. When the danger of frost has past, harden off the plant in a cold frame before planting outdoors.

Hardy ferns in baskets and rafts will benefit from being over-wintered in cold frames. Keep the soil barely moist and remove decaying fronds. If limitations of space prevent over-wintering in cold-frames, baskets or rafts should be placed in a shaded, sheltered area. Keep decayed fronds on the fern to give some shelter to the next season's growth. In spring, when the new growth emerges, remove the remains of the previous year's fronds, apply a weak organic fertilizer, and water thoroughly.

Tender species cultivated in sub-tropical climates can be over-wintered in cold frames or shaded, sheltered areas. Keep the basket barely moist and remove any weak growth that emerges during this time. In spring apply an organic fertilizer. Resume watering and return the basket to its garden site.

Ferns for outdoor baskets and rafts

(★ indicates hardy fern, *see* p. 51)

Adiantum caudatum, A. cuneatum, A. gracillimum, A. Moorei, Asplenium belangeri, A. longissimum, A. viviparum, Davallia canariensis, D. denticulata, D. fejeensis, D. mariesii, D. pallida, Humata tyermannii, Nephrolepis cordifolia vars., *N. acuminata* vars., *N. exaltata* vars., *Pellaea atropurpurea*★, *P. brachyptera, P. falcata, P. rotundifolia, Platycerium* spp., *Polypodium* spp., *Polypodium australe*★, *P. vulgare*★, *Pyrrosia lingua.*

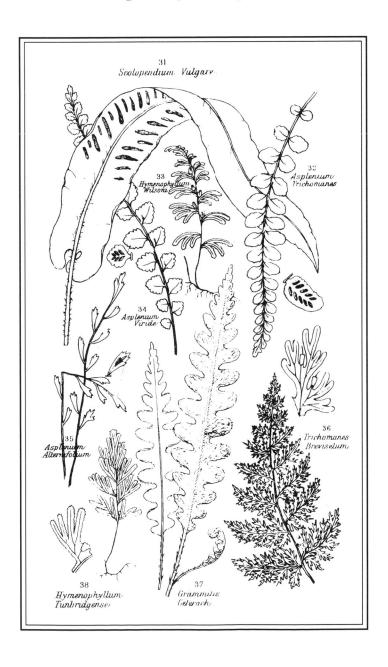

6

GROWING FERNS IN LARGER GARDENS

There can be few large gardens which can afford to forgo the longlasting and ever developing beauty of the fern. Possessing a lingering appeal, ferns transcend the briefer season of many other plants. Ascending from the warming earth in early spring, with clusters of vibrant green croziers, they provide through the heat of summer days oases of cool verdure. In autumn, their russet-tinged fronds intimate shortening days and winter's approach.

FERNS IN FLOWER BEDS AND BORDERS

The durability of the fern's display can be used to provide islands of stability and permanent interest in the seasonally-changing flowerscape of the mixed, herbaceous border. A monochrome of green, the ferns' foliage will provide both contrast and a restful interlude in the kaleidoscopic display of flowering plants such as *Papaver*, *Hibiscus*, lupin and other perennials.

To show to full advantage, larger ferns should be given enough room to develop their fronds unhindered by surrounding plants. The habits of the ferns selected will dictate the space required. Those with erect, shuttlecock fronds will need less space than those with arching fronds. Ferns with erect fronds, such as *Athyrium* and most *Dryopteris* species, should be given up to three foot around the plant. Ferns of more spreading habit, such as *Onoclea* and *Osmunda* species will need at least one third more space. Trunk-forming arboreal ferns, such as *Dicksonia*, *Cyathea* and some *Blechnum* species, will need less space as they develop height. In very mild temperate areas and warmer climates tree ferns create spectacular focal points in large borders and island beds, lending an exotic charm to the most commonplace planting scheme.

The bed's exposure to sun will place some limitations on the species of ferns to be chosen. In very sunny sites it is important to provide the best possible soil conditions. An open soil, rich in humus, will help preserve sufficient moisture around the ferns' roots. In such a potentially difficult site for ferns, some form of additional watering will be necessary throughout spring and summer.

Among the larger ferns, those within the genera *Athyrium*, *Dryopteris*, *Onoclea* and *Osmunda* will prove the most satisfactory in these sites. Smaller ferns, such as those in the genera *Cheilanthes*, *Ceterach*, *Blechnum*, *Pellaea* and *Polypodium* can also be accommodated where more compact plants are required. Ferns with long creeping rhizomes do not lend themselves to bedding schemes, except the most informal sort. The spreading habit of their rootstock – invaluable in situations where attractive ground cover is needed – does not allow the necessary degree of predictability in their arrangement in the border display.

A moist, well-drained site will allow chosen species to develop to advantage in this location. Where large ferns are planted against the shelter of a wall, as a backdrop for flowering plants, they may not receive sufficient water. Although the shade cast by other plants will help to reduce the evaporation of moisture from the soil around the roots of the ferns, some form of permanent irrigation will allow an adequate supply of moisture to these thirsty sites. Herbaceous borders, where the area is fairly extensive, will benefit from semi-automatic watering via inexpensive plastic pipes, perforated at intervals along their length, laid inconspicuously along the perimeter of the bed. Wide beds may require further pipes sunk across the bed.

Perennial borders need to be well prepared prior to planting. Double digging, with the addition of well-rotted organic matter, is a prerequisite for the successful herbaceous border, ensuring the necessary degree of moisture retention and nutrient supply.

The flowering plants of the border will require additional feeding throughout the summer. A slow-release fertilizer, which will not burn the roots of the ferns, should be applied at monthly intervals. Reduce feeding in late summer and do not feed after mid-autumn. A mulch of leafmould and peat, three or four inches in depth, applied in late autumn will replenish the soil and assist soil warming in spring.

In warmer climates, where perennial plants are less successful in borders or beds, annuals tend to be chosen for these locations. Many of the larger ferns would be out of keeping with the more modest scale of annual plants. However the reduction in the stature of ferns for these beds does not impede the variety of effects that can be created using smaller ferns.

Beds which have poor soils, or where annual bedding is employed, suggest the use of pot-grown ferns. These can be planted in the soil up to the rim of the pot in chosen locations. This type of cultivation offers the advantage of allowing semi-tender and tender species to be grown in temperate regions. It also permits the siting of ferns to be modified to comply with the changing decorative demands of the bed, as one flush of annuals succeeds another.

Although the soil around the pot will prevent excessive moisture loss, the pots will have to be watered individually. Where frosts can be expected in winter, pots containing semi-tender and tender ferns should be removed in early autumn to the shelter of a heated greenhouse, or indoors, where minimum temperatures of 50–60°F (10–16°C) can be maintained.

Where colour is required throughout the year, evergreen species should be chosen. In warm climates many ferns will keep their fronds intact throughout the year. In colder climes, the hardy species of fern from Japan give an evergreen display. In spring, the previous year's fronds can be removed before they hinder the young growth then emerging.

In temperate regions, hardy, deciduous ferns can be relied upon to give superb autumn colour, their fronds gradually mellowing from vivid green to gold, copper, burnt orange and deepest brown. During winter dormancy, the old fronds can be left on the plant to offer new tissue some protection. In spring, when the new flush of growth emerges, the old fronds should be cut off cleanly one inch above the crowns with a sharp knife.

An attractive, low-maintenance alternative to traditional summer bedding schemes can be created using one or more species of the low-growing forms of fern. *Athyrium distentifolium* (alpine lady fern), most *Cheilanthes*, *Gymnocarpium dryopteris* (oak fern), *Phegopteris connectilis* (beech fern), and *Pteris* species would produce a cool, elegant display in those deeply shaded areas which are less than ideal for most flowering plants.

Ferns for beds and borders (⋆ indicates hardy fern, *see* p. 51)

Medium ferns 24–36in. (60–90cm)

Athyrium filix-femina⋆, *A. goeringianum*⋆, *A. thelypteroides*⋆, *A. pycnocarpon*, *Blechnum spicant*⋆, *B. tabulare*, *Cheilanthes* spp., *Cyrtomium falcatum*, *Dryopteris* spp.⋆, *Nephrolepis* spp., *Pellaea atropurpurea*⋆, *Pellaea* spp. *Polystichum* spp.⋆.

Large ferns

Blechnum braziliense, *B. gibbum*, *Cibotium* spp., *Cyathea* spp., *Dicksonia antarctica*, *Dicksonia* spp., *Diplazium* spp., *Matteuccia pensylvanica*⋆, *M. struthiopteris*⋆, *Onoclea sensibilis*⋆, *Osmunda* spp.⋆, *Woodwardia* spp.⋆.

PLANTING FERNS IN ALPINE BEDS AND ROCK GARDENS

Alpine beds and rockeries provide ready-made locations for fern planting. Genuine alpine beds, devoted to plants from high, generally dry temperate regions, will require, if congruity is to be maintained, a selection of ferns associated with mountain and upland areas.

In well-drained, peaty soil with a good content of organic nutrients, ferns of dwarf habit will blend sympathetically with such calcifuge genera as *Aquilegia*, *Gentiana* (some), *Pulsatilla*, *Saxifraga* and *Scilla*. A choice can be made from the smaller *Blechnum* species, *Cryptogramma crispa* (parsley fern), *Gymnocarpium dryopteris* (oak fern), *Phegopteris connectilis* (beech fern) and *Woodsia*. These are compact, low-growing species which will thrive in damp peaty conditions. If a taller plant would be more in keeping with established bedding, then *Athyrium distentifolium* (alpine lady fern), or *Polystichum setiferum* would be ideal.

In an alkaline bed, host to flowering plants such as those from the genera *Alyssum*, *Aubrietia*, *Campanula* and *Helianthemum*, choose small hardy ferns such as *Adiantum venustum*, *Athyrium distentifolium*, *Polypodium* species, *Phyllitis scolopendrium* (hart's tongue), *Cheilanthes*, *Cystopteris fragilis* (brittle bladder fern), *Polystichum aculeatum*, *Polystichum lonchitis* (holly fern) and the various species of *Asplenium*.

A scree bed, slightly alkaline, composed of stone chippings or slate with little humus, would be a particularly good site for the planting of ferns which prefer a very free-draining site. Of the hardy ferns the evergreen *Polystichum lonchitis* (holly fern), *Gymnocarpium robertianum* (limestone oak fern), *Dryopteris submontana* syn. *D. villarii* (limestone buckler) and *Polypodium australe* (southern polypody) will find conditions in this site closely matching those of their native habitats.

Alpine beds are rarely successful in warmer regions, partly because of the absence of the prolonged frosts needed to promote dormancy. In areas of high rainfall, outdoor alpine beds often fail to repay the care invested in them, despite good drainage and careful cultivation. Where success with true alpines cannot be obtained, rockeries are best devoted to small indigenous species. A bed composed of free-draining, leafy soil, and planted with compact-flowering species of woodland, rocky wastes and marginal land, makes an ideal mini-habitat for small semi-tender and tender ferns. Native, compact species of such genera as *Anemone*, *Aquilegia*, *Campanula*, *Dianthus*, *Geranium*, *Primula* and *Viola*, when combined with smaller indigenous fern species, will provide a planting scheme to rival the gracefulness of those plants of higher altitudes.

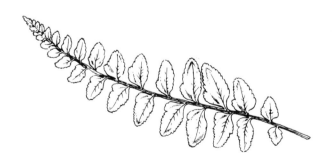

Feeding and watering

A well prepared alpine bed which is sheltered from full sun should require little additional watering or feeding. Most alpine plants are adapted to short periods of semi-drought and will survive and prosper on the moisture received from rainfall. Certainly, overwatering and the application of excessive fertilizer will generate stagnant conditions leading to root-rot and fungal attacks. However, those rockery beds devoted to indigenous plants may need more moisture than those where true alpine plants are grown.

FERN COLONIES AND ACID AND ALKALINE SOIL

One particularly attractive way of growing and displaying ferns is to create fern colonies where individual, or compatible species can be given areas within the garden. Given sufficient garden space, areas could be designated for both acid and alkaline soil. Although this may sound daunting, in a small area it is both simple and inexpensive.

Acid-loving genera such as *Athyrium*, *Blechnum*, *Cryptogramma*, *Dryopteris*, *Oreopteris* and *Thelypteris* can be accommodated in raised beds made of peat blocks standing 12 to 18 inches above the surrounding soil. The planting medium should be composed of equal parts of fine gravel, lime-free peat and leafmould. It is important to site the beds in a very shady spot as these ferns are intolerant of drought.

An alkaline raised bed can be constructed on the same principle, using limestone blocks to enclose the bed. Garden soil enriched with leafmould and limestone chippings will be a satisfactory planting medium. Over the seasons some leaching of the soil will take place, so additional lime must be added when required. Soil testing will help determine the pH of the soil and the necessary corrections to be made to retain the alkalinity. Here can be grown species within the genera *Asplenium*, *Cheilanthes*, *Hemionitis*, *Notholaena*, *Pellaea*, *Pteris* and *Tectaria*. Tropical and semi-tropical species of these genera can be grown outdoors even in temperate regions if they are treated as temporary plantings. In autumn remove the plants to indoor locations sheltered from winter frosts.

VERTICAL GARDENS

Shaded walls and rocky terracing lend themselves easily to those ferns which can thrive in crevices. These ferns can be used to add interest to an old wall by implanting small specimens, together with a little peat or fern compost, into crevices in the mortar. In temperate climates, suitable ferns include the hardy *Asplenium* species, *Polypodium vulgare*, *Phyllitis scolopendrium* (hart's tongue), *Cystopteris fragilis* (brittle bladder fern) and *Ceterach officinarum* (rusty-back fern). The choice of species will be determined by the scale of the wall and its exposure to sun. For a sheltered wall choose *Cystopteris fragilis*, *Asplenium ruta-muraria*, *A. trichomanes* and the several *Woodsia* species. A large wall with good shade will also support colonies of *Athyrium filix-femina*, *Phyllitis scolopendrium* and *Polypodium*. For walls exposed to full sun choose *Ceterach officinarum* or the semi-hardy species of *Cheilanthes*. Until they are seen to establish their roots, watering in dry weather will be a wise precaution. In urban areas, the ferns will benefit from an occasional hosing down to wash off the inevitable accumulated pollution. In warmer climates, which will allow the planting of semi-tropical and tropical epiphytes, it is possible to carpet a large wall completely with these ferns.

Whilst an open-textured, dry-stone wall presents a ready-made site for a vertical garden, a plain mortared brick wall can be exploited to support a low, dry-stone wall, which can be host to a rich variety of ferns.

Start by measuring out the extent of the proposed retaining wall. The two factors which will restrict the scale of the wall are the weight of material bearing on the original wall, and the amount of rock you can obtain for the new wall. As a general guide, the new wall should only be half the height of the supporting wall. To prevent dampness encroaching on the brickwork of the mortared wall it may be prudent to line it with stout polythene sheeting.

Start by excavating a trench, one foot deep, at a distance of three feet from the wall. This trench will form the foundations for the new wall. Place the first layer of large stones along the trench, tilting the stones at a 30 degree angle to the vertical. Fill in the gap between the old and new wall with small stones and rubble. Compact the infill to eradicate any air pockets and to minimize the possibility of settling at a later stage. Continue in the same manner for the next and succeeding layers, making sure that you keep the stones fairly even across the length of the wall. To ensure stability, the new wall should incline inwards towards the original wall. The gaps between the stones should be well filled with a gritty soil mix and small stones. The top 12 inches should be infilled with a mixture of excavated loam, leafmould and grit.

The top of the wall will provide the acid conditions suitable for a variety of fern species: *Blechnum*, *Athyrium*, and the smaller *Dryopteris* species would all find this a congenial site. Alternatively, a choice could be made from amongst those ferns with creeping rhizomes such as hardy *Polypodium*, *Gymnocarpium dryopteris*, and *Phegopteris connectilis*. In suitable climates the tender species of *Actinopteris*, *Cheilanthes*, *Davallia* and *Pyrrosia* will quickly colonize the site.

On the face of the wall, smaller, winter-green ferns can be planted in the crevices, which will have been prepared by the addition of small amounts of gritty humus. Pack the humus well into crevices, leaving no gaps which will trap air. Take young pot-grown specimens out of their containers, removing surplus soil from around the roots, and carefully insert each fern in its crevice so that the crown is just exposed. Fill around the plant with more humus. If planted at an angle of 45 degrees, rainwater will percolate down to the roots. A colony of ferns made up of *Phyllitis scolopendrium*, *Cystopteris fragilis*, *Polypodium* and *Asplenium*, including the *A. ruta-muraria* (wall rue), *A. viride* (green spleenwort) and *A. adiantum nigrum* (black spleenwort) will, over a period of years, colonize the area, making an evergreen carpet. In a more open aspect, *Ceterach officinarum* (rusty-back fern) or *Asplenium trichomanes* (maidenhair spleenwort) will prove to be more tolerant of exposure to sun.

The soil around the base of the wall will have become compacted during the construction of the wall. It will need to be re-dug adding plenty of leafmould and leftover small stones. The resulting soil mix will provide a perfect medium for larger moisture-loving ferns such as *Osmunda regalis*, *Matteuccia struthiopteris*, *Dryopteris aemula*, *D. dilatata*, and *Onoclea sensibilis*.

Vertical gardens without walls

The absence of a wall need not prevent the creation of a decorative and unusual vertical garden. A moss and leafmould wall, can be simply and inexpensively erected. To make this structure (which would be an ideal site for a wide variety of ferns), a skeleton frame of timber should be constructed to the required dimensions. The base should be supported by heavy planks of wood, or old railway sleepers. This will retain the compost at the bottom and stabilize the overall structure. The whole frame should be covered with narrow-gauge nylon bird netting. The lower part of the interior can be filled with a mix of leafmould, loam and limestone chippings. This will provide a suitable alkaline medium for *Asplenium*, *Cystopteris* and smaller *Polystichum* species. The upper part of the framework is filled with a mixture of leafmould, loam and grit. This will provide the neutral-to-acidic soil which will suit the more compact varieties *Athyrium*, *Dryopteris* and *Blechnum*. To plant individual ferns, the netting is cut sufficiently to allow the plant to be inserted. As the plants develop more of the netting round the individual ferns can be cut to allow the fronds to emerge without hindrance.

Ferns for walls to 12in. (30cm) (★ indicates hardy fern, *see* p. 51)

Actinopteris australis, *Adiantum capillus-veneris*, *Anogramma chaerophylla*, *Asplenium adiantum-nigrum*★, *A. ruta-muraria*★, *A. trichomanes*★, *A. viride*★, *Athyrium distentifolium*★, *A. goeringianum* 'Pictum'★, *Camptosorus rhizophyllus*, *Ceterach aureum*, *C. officinarum*★, *Cheilanthes* spp., *Cystopteris alpina*★, *C. bulbifera*, *C. dickieana*★, *C. fragilis*★, *C. montana*★, *Cyrtomium falcatum*, *Dryopteris affinis*★, *D. austriaca*★, *D. sieboldii*, *Gymnocarpium robertianum*★, *Phyllitis scolopendrium* vars.★, *Polypodium* spp., *Polystichum* spp.★, *Woodsia glabella*★.

Plate 1
Osmunda regalis (royal fern) and the invasive aquatic *Equisetum fluviatile* (water horsetail) in early summer

Plate 2
Oreopteris limbosperma (sweet mountain fern) requires the moist acid soil found within the pool margins

Plate 3 *(opposite)*
The fronds of *Osmunda
regalis* are translucent in
the early morning June
sunlight. *Polygonum
bistorta* 'Superbum' and
Primula provide
background interest

Plate 4 *(above left)*
Dryopteris filix-mas (male
fern), *Phyllitis
scolopendrium* (hart's
tongue fern) and *Athyrium
filix-femina* (lady fern)

Plate 5 *(above right)*
Verbena, Iberis and *Ajuga
reptens* provide a colourful
backdrop to *Athyrium
filix-femina foliosum
grandiceps*

Plate 6 *(right)*
Dryopteris filix-mas,
together with a plumose
variety of *Polystichum
setiferum* (soft shield fern)
thrive under the shade
cast by *Acer platanoides*

Plate 9
Weathered rockwork in dappled shade provides a congenial site for a variety of hardy ferns

Plate 10
The poolside planting of *Osmunda cinnamomea* (cinnamon fern) provides a strong contrast to *Acer palmatum* 'Dissectum Atropurpureum'

Plate 11
Athyrium filix-femina corymbiferum is an extreme example of the many crested varieties of lady fern

Plate 12
Planted in a moist soil, by late June the fronds of this mature *Matteuccia struthiopteris* (shuttlecock fern) have grown to six feet (two metres)

Plate 13
The moisture–loving *Onoclea sensibilis* (sensitive fern) thrives in this location. Its sterile fronds will turn brown at the first frost

Plate 14
Athyrium filix-femina, Astilbe, Hosta and *Primula* luxuriate in the moist, streamside soil

Plate 17
The extensive creeping rhizomes of *Gymnocarpium dryopteris* (oak fern) have allowed it to colonize this bank created from rock and peat blocks

Plate 18
Athyrium filix-femina, *Meconopsis cambrica* (Welsh poppy) and *Aquilegia* (columbine) have exploited crannies and crevices between boulders, softening the contours of the garden path

Plate 19
In July, the clumps of
Athyrium filix-femina
provide a foil for Harlow
Car's celebrated display of
candelabra *Primula*

Plate 20
The stolons trailing from
this plumose variety of
Nephrolepis exaltata offer
an easy means of
increasing stock

Plate 21
Logs have been used here to good effect to support a number of exotic plants within this Wardian case. *Lygodium japonicum* (Japanese climbing fern) entwines itself between the insectivorous *Nepenthes* (pitcher plant). The fronds of *Adiantum hispidulum* (rosy maidenhair) will lose their pink tinge as the season progresses

Plate 22
The velvet-like patches at the tips of the fertile fronds of *Platycerium bifurcatum* (stag's horn fern) contain the sporangia

Plate 23 (left)
Ceratopteris thalictroides
(water sprite) can be
grown as a free–floating
aquatic or rooted in
shallow mud

Plate 24 (above left)
Adiantum hispidulum,
A. capillus-veneris and
A. peruvianum illustrate
the variation of frond
texture to be found in the
Adiantum genus. The
waxy fronds of
A. hispidulum indicate a
greater tolerance to low
humidity

Plate 25 (above right)
A native of thickets and
open woods, *Lygodium
japonicum* exploits
surrounding trees and
shrubs as support

Plate 26 (right)
Dicksonia squarrosa and
Woodwardia radicans

Plate 27
Dicksonia antarctica and
D. squarrosa were brought
from New Zealand in the
nineteenth century to
stock the conservatory at
Tatton

Plate 28
Under *Begonia haageana*
the soft, feathery foliage
of *Sellaginella Martensii*
provides effective ground
cover

Plate 29
Dwarfed by *Victoria cruziana* (giant waterlily), *Ceratopteris thalictroides*, *Regnelidium diphyllum* and *Nephrolepis exaltata* soften the edges of the conservatory pool

Plate 30
The plantlets growing on the surface of the fronds of *Asplenium bulbiferum* (mother and child fern) are a source of perennial interest. They provide an easy means of increasing stock

Plate 31
Like many of the large hardy ferns, *Oreopteris limbosperma* adds interest to well-established shrub borders

Plate 32
The fronds of *Phyllitis scolopendrium* will grow to 2 feet (60cm) in this moist, partly shaded site

Plate 33
Polypodium vulgare bifidum
will remain evergreen
throughout the winter

Plate 34
Dryopteris filix-mas
luxuriates in a moist
shaded site

Plate 35
By late summer the fronds of *Athyrium filix-femina foliosum grandiceps* are turning gold

Plate 36
The massed planting of the hardy *Matteuccia struthiopteris* provides stunning ground cover on a moist riverbank

Plate 37
Osmunda regalis croziers in spring

Plate 38
Osmunda regalis and *Dryopteris filix-mas* lend enchantment to this Japanese garden

Plate 39 *(above left)*
The distinctive *Osmunda Claytonia* (interrupted fern) bears spores on fertile leaflets midway along its fronds

Plate 40 *(above right)*
Phyllitis scolopendrium crispum nobile is one of many varieties of this species

Plate 41 *(left)*
Many hardy ferns luxuriate in the moist and shaded conditions to be found along this riverbank

Plate 42 *(right)*
A native of the Himalayas, *Adiantum venustum* is a hardy, deciduous species suited to the larger rock garden

Plate 43
The vivid green of *Oreopteris limbosperma* contrasts with the sombre tones of overhanging shrubs

Plate 44
A mature *Dryopteris oreades* (mountain male fern) during June, showing the characteristic accumulation of multiple crowns

Plate 47
Dryopteris dilatata (broad
buckler fern) is
widespread in European
deciduous woodlands

Plate 48
The carpet of *Geranium
dalmaticum* is a colourful
backdrop to *Dryopteris
filix-mas* 'Cristata'

PLANTING UNDER TREES

Many ferns are best suited to planting in areas which are shaded from full sun during summer. The cover provided by a canopy of established trees can prove to be a good location for these species of fern. Typically hosts to the spring-time displays of crocus, daffodil and other bulbs, these areas are generally the most under-exploited part of any garden. With a little care in the planting of young ferns, the established colonies of bulbs can be left undisturbed. Bare areas to be planted with ferns will benefit from being dug over and a generous amount of rotted leafmould and grit added to the soil. This will help ensure a spongy, moisture-retentive soil in an area which will receive less rainfall when the canopy of leaf closes over the patch in summer.

In grassed areas under trees, and where bulbs are already established, there is less opportunity to prepare the soil. Here the gardener will have to compromise. After removing enough grass to provide space for the ferns, dig out the soil below and replace it with a mix of leafmould and grit. Preference in this site should be given to deciduous and drought-tolerant species. The fronds of the ferns will emerge after the bulbs have flowered, disguising the rather untidy foliage of the bulbous plants, allowing the site to be visually interesting for most of the year.

Young specimens have a better chance of establishing themselves than more mature ferns. Some additional watering will be necessary while the plants adapt to conditions in this demanding site.

The species of fern to choose in these areas will depend on the scale of tree planting and the soil conditions. In open-textured soils any of the woodland ferns will prosper. Three or four specimens of *Athyrium* under small, isolated trees would provide an elegant counterpoint to the leaves and branches of the trees. A collection of more mature trees would allow the planting of a wider range of ferns including *Athyrium*, *Dryopteris* and *Polystichum* species. A scree soil would be more in keeping for *Diplazium pycnocarpon*, *Polystichum lonchitis* or *Dryopteris submontana*.

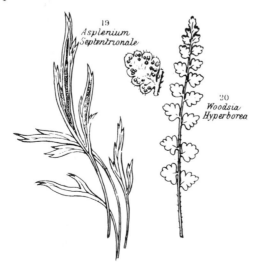

19
Asplenium Septentrionale

20
Woodsia Hyperborea

Areas of high rainfall and the moist basins of sloping sites, where the soil will be predominantly acid, are ideal for *Blechnum*, *Diplazium*, *Dryopteris*, *Matteuccia* and *Thelypteris*. These ferns will reach two to three feet in height. More compact ferns which have a spreading habit are *Polystichum setiferum* (soft shield fern), *Phegopteris connectilis* (beech fern), and *Gymnocarpium dryopteris* (oak fern).

For alkaline soils choose *Polystichum aculeatum* (hard shield fern), *Polystichum lonchitis* (holly fern), *Phyllitis scolopendrium* (hart's tongue), *Gymnocarpium robertianum* (limestone oak fern) and *Dryopteris submontana* (limestone buckler fern).

PLANTING ALONGSIDE POOLS AND STREAMS

A traditional and very elegant planting site for some of the larger, luxuriant ferns is by the side of a pool. The most obvious choice for this would be *Osmunda regalis* (royal fern). Two or three of these plants would, over a few years, make an imposing garden feature, reaching three to four feet in height after only a few years. Some specimens can, after many years, measure up to five feet wide. Other ferns for planting alongside pools or streams include *Osmunda cinnamomea* (cinnamon fern), *Osmunda claytoniana* (interrupted fern), *Matteuccia struthiopteris* (shuttlecock fern), *Onoclea sensibilis* (sensitive fern) and *Oreopteris limbosperma* (sweet mountain fern). *Matteuccia struthiopteris* is a particularly fine fern which produces graceful, crested plumes three to four feet long. A group of these ferns planted by the bank of a stream makes a most impressive display.

BOG GARDENS

The absence of a pool need not prevent the cultivation of moisture-loving ferns. The base of a sloping piece of garden, providing it is sufficiently shady, is an ideal spot for the construction of a bog garden. The scale of the bog area will depend on the individual garden, but even a medium-sized garden will benefit from having such a feature, since it will greatly extend the range of plant cultivation.

A basin–shape, with a graduated incline towards the edges, would allow for a variation in the moisture-retentiveness of the bog area, the central section being the most moist and the perimeter becoming drier. This would allow scope for a variety of soil conditions within a relatively small area, and a correspondingly varied plant community.

Although the task of excavating the soil can seem an unattractive prospect, the planning stages at any rate can be done with little effort. These will include mapping out the area with a cordon and purchasing a suitable liner for the base. For a large bog, several yards across, it may be worthwhile employing a local contractor to manage the heavy work of excavating, laying the liner and infilling the excavated topsoil. A compact area could be attempted without specialist equipment but with the help of some friends.

After excavating the soil to the required depth and width, it is a simple matter to lay the liner. To ensure that the soil in the central portion does not become sour with stagnant water, lightly pierce the liner with a fork to provide a little drainage. All that is then required is to infill with topsoil, mixed with a good quantity of rotted leafmould and peat. Some generosity with the peat and leafmould will help to create the acidity in the soil which is essential for many bog plants.

Soak pot-grown ferns overnight before removing them from their pots and planting them in the soil. It will be more practical to complete as much of the planting as possible before adding water to the site. The water needed to create the bog should be added gradually. It may be prudent to under-water initially, topping up over a period of weeks until optimum conditions have been achieved. Depending on climatic factors there may be no need to replenish the water levels artificially. In dry areas, artificial irrigation could be incorporated at the design stage to sustain the moisture level.

Ferns for poolside planting and within boggy areas
(* indicates hardy fern, *see* p. 51)

Ferns of medium height 24–36in. (60–90cm)

Adiantum tenerum, A. trapeziforme, Anemia adiantifolia, A. phyllitidis, Athyrium spp., Blechnum auriculatum★, B. patersonii, B. tabulare★, Davallia canariensis, D. solida, Dryopteris spp., Equisetum variegata, Leptopteris superba, Matteuccia pensylvanica★, M. struthiopteris★, Nephrolepis spp., Oreopteris limbosperma★, Thelypteris decursive-pinnata, T. dentata, T. phegopteris★, Woodwardia areolata★, W. orientalis★, W. radicans★.

Large ferns

Acrostichum aureum, Aglaomorpha spp., Anopteris hexagona, Blechnum brasiliense, B. gibbum, Cibotium spp., Cyathea australis, C. dealbata, Marattia fraxinea, Microlepia spp., Osmunda claytoniana★, O. regalis★, Stenochlaena palustris, Todea barbara.

CREATING A WILD GARDEN

A particularly welcome trend in gardening circles has been the revival of interest in native species of plants. Much neglected in the recent past, in favour of more exotic and pest-prone hybrids, the virtues of native flowering plants are becoming more widely appreciated. Not as obvious and gaudy as their hybrid cousins, the wild flowers have an understated charm which has lasting appeal.

Within the larger garden, the combination of indigenous ferns and wild flowers could create a series of authentic miniature habitats. This type of project would not only be aesthetically pleasing but would also be a valuable contribution to maintaining these dwindling species.

The creation of a wild garden can rarely be achieved quickly, and some setbacks can be expected. Occasionally, the chosen plants will fail to adapt to garden conditions. Generally, this is due to incompatible soil conditions. In other cases it may be due to climatic factors, where the plants have been extended too far beyond their natural geographic boundaries. The most successful wild gardens are those where local species are chosen and where the planting is sympathetic to indigenous habitats.

Some advance planning will be necessary before embarking on the venture. Although garden conditions can be adapted, with ingenuity and effort, to accommodate all native plants, it may prove more expedient initially to evaluate the present site and adopt those plants which will prosper in the existing soil conditions.

The first task is to survey the site in some detail. If the soil structure is unfamiliar some assessment of it should be made. Where the garden is large, there may be local variations of soil structure which will assist in creating a variety of habitats. Mounds and natural depressions can be an asset, creating areas of miniature banks and gullies in which different species will prosper. Similarly, existing walls, sheltered hedges and paths can be host to many native plants.

The results of the survey should be incorporated into a plan. A map of the garden showing existing features, soil conditions and shade-cover will allow you to get an over-view of how the garden may be developed.

If only part of the garden is to be given over to native ferns and wild flowers it will be best to use the least fertile site for the native plant area. In contrast to hybrid forms, most wild plant species prefer a low-fertility soil.

Obtaining plants

When your plans have been formulated and your list of chosen wildflowers has been made, then it is time to obtain the plants. For the most part your collection will start off as seed. Some seed could be collected by hand in late summer and autumn from local sites if the more common wild plants are to be chosen. This has the advantage that your own soil conditions are likely to be compatible with the species. However, careless harvesting and over-collection of seed can lead to a decline in local plant populations. A further handicap for the harvester is that the collection of seed from many wild flowers is illegal.

Fortunately, there are now many nurseries specializing in wild flower seed. These nurseries are by far the best solution to establishing garden colonies of wild plants of all but the most common species.

A great mistake that is made by many new to this form of gardening, is to sow the seeds of native, hardy plants in a heated greenhouse. Most species, particularly annuals, native to temperate Europe and N. America, can be sown directly onto the site, providing that they are not exposed to soggy ground conditions or the drying winds which will rob the seedlings of essential moisture.

If you are unsure of the optimum growing conditions for the species, or where perennial wild plants are to be grown, the seeds may be sown in pans and trays shortly after they are harvested. The container should have a layer of coarse grit, stones and crocks to provide good drainage. Fill the container to within half an inch of the rim with a commercial seed compost or a mix of one part coarse sand, one part peat, two parts loam. Water the compost thoroughly and leave to drain before sowing the seeds. Sow thinly and to a depth equal to their thickness. Sprinkle compost lightly over the soil and cover the container with a sheet of glass or polythene. Place it in a shady spot outdoors or in a cold frame. When the seeds have germinated, remove the cover and allow them to grow on for a week or two before pricking out and planting in individual pots.

In preparing the compost for individual potted plants, better growth characteristics will be achieved by attempting to emulate the soil characteristics of the plant's native habitat. Plants of rocky terrain should be given a free-draining compost, containing coarse grit or gravel. Where a species is known to prefer alkaline conditions, add limestone chippings to the compost. Before they are planted into their final sites the young plants should be hardened off by being exposed gradually to outdoor conditions. This can be achieved by raising the covers of cold frames for increasingly long periods during the day. When they are completely hardened off, generally after two or three weeks of this treatment, the plants are ready for planting in the chosen garden site. Perennials will benefit from spending one year in a nursery bed where pots can be sunk in plunge beds containing a sand and soil mix.

Before young plants are transferred to the open garden they should be watered well. Remove the plant from the pot, disturbing the roots as little as possible. Excavate the soil sufficiently to make space for the rootball and compost. The plant should be placed in the ground to the same depth to which it occupied its pot. Fill in around the plant with excavated soil, pressing firmly to exclude air pockets. Water the plant and the surrounding soil. Until the plant becomes established and a good root system is developed, additional watering will be required during the spring and summer months.

Walls and paths

The simplest way to sample the charms of wild flower gardening is to devote one area of the garden to that type of planting. To minimize disruption to established garden schemes a suitable area such as rock-work, open-textured stone walls or gravel paths could be selected for a first essay in wild flower gardening. Most wild flowering plants adapted to these situations will need the minimum of attention after planting, and will provide a perennial source of colour and interest.

While many ferns adapted to rocky ground and scree soils prefer shady conditions, the flowering plants of these soils will appreciate a sunnier location. Where there is some variability in the shade cover within these sites, the more open conditions can be given over to the flowering plants. However, to complement the flowering plants grown in sunny spots, *Asplenium ruta-muraria*, *A. trichomanes*, all *Cheilanthes* species, *Ceterach officinarum* and *Polypodium* species can be relied upon to survive and prosper in relatively exposed, sunny areas.

Walls or rock-work provide a natural site for those flowering plants and ferns which prefer dry conditions around their roots. If introduced into loamy soil, the constant moisture around the roots would encourage rot. The fissures and crannies of an open-textured, rock-work allow the plants a cool root run and access to sufficient moisture percolating through crevices. Like ferns such as *Asplenium*, *Cheilanthes*, *Polypodium* and *Woodsia*, many flowering plants of dry and rocky soils will find the moisture trapped between the stones sufficient in all but the driest periods.

Choose small specimens for such sites. Large plants can be divided to provide a number of smaller plants. Periodic division will be necessary in any case as most rock-growing flowering plants, generally referred to as chasmophytes, are short lived, reproducing rapidly either by seed or vegetatively by offsets. The procedure for planting flowering species is the same as for small ferns. If the plant has been growing in a container, water it thoroughly an hour or so before removing it from the pot. You will need to remove most of the soil from the plant, ensuring that its roots are not damaged in the process. Select a suitable crevice in the wall which will house the plant. The crevice should be just large enough to accommodate the roots, together with a small amount of soil. Where planting on the face of a wall, try to insert the plant at an angle of 45 degrees. This will allow rainwater and other precipitation to flow down the stem to the roots. Insert the plant carefully, with the growing point or crown just proud of the crevice. Pack around the roots a gritty soil mixed with a little leafmould or peat, ensuring that any air pockets, which would dry out the roots, are removed. Secure the soil with splinters of rock. Water the plant thoroughly, avoiding washing away the soil around the roots.

Where rock-work is not available, other areas of the garden can be exploited. Gravel paths or areas of scree are an alternative site for those plants which prefer a free-draining soil. Where areas of scree are being created within the garden, the soil should be composed of at least 50 per cent chippings, with the remaining 50 per cent made up of an equal mix of sandy loam and leafmould. To ensure good drainage in areas of heavy soil, excavate six inches of topsoil and replace with a layer of cinders or brick rubble. Alternatively, a sloping portion of the garden can be chosen as the scree site. The latter option will produce the most natural effect and may not require a layer of artificial drainage. Perennial plants for such sites might include the members of the *Chrysosplenium* (saxifrage), *Sedum* (stonecrop), *Dianthus* (pinks), *Alyssum*, and *Geranium* families. These plants are native to rocky or shallow soils.

Although small ferns with erect or ascending crowns are most associated with this type of location, other species with creeping rhizomes such as *Cheilanthes*, *Onychium* and *Pteris* can be planted where they can establish a satisfactory root-run. In frost-prone climates the hardy *Gymnocarpium robertianum* (limestone oak fern) and *Polypodium australe*'s creeping rhizomes will colonize rock-work and scree beds.

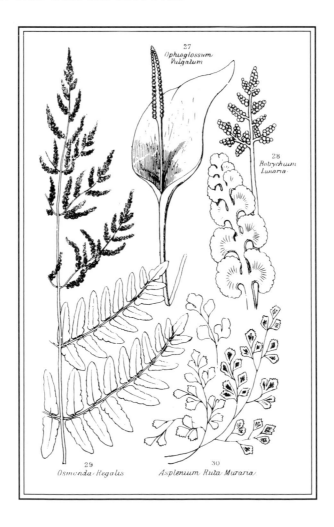

Suggested perennial flowering plants for open-textured walls:

Alyssum saxatile, 4–12in. (10–30cm), yellow flowers in spring, Europe.

Anagallis arvensis (scarlet pimpernel), 3–12in. (8–30cm), scarlet flowers in summer, Europe and N. America.

Aster alpinus, 4–9in. (10–23cm), blue flowers in summer, N. America.

Chelidonium majus (greater celandine), 12–36in. (30–90cm), yellow flowers in summer, Europe and N. America.

Dianthus gratianopolitanus, 4–12in. (10–30cm), pink flowers in spring, Europe.

Dryas Drummondii, 3in. (8cm), yellow flowers in summer, N. America.

Dryas octopetala (mountain avens), spread 18in. (46cm), white flowers in spring, Europe and N. America.

Gentiana clusii (stemless trumpet gentian), 1–6in. (2–15cm), blue flowers in spring, Europe.

Gentiana verna (spring gentian), 1–6in. (2–15cm), blue flowers in spring, Europe.

Gentiana calycosa, 12in. (30cm), blue flowers in summer, N. America.

Geranium robertianum (herb robert), 4–20in. (10–51cm), pink flowers in summer, Europe and N. America.

Geranium sanguineum (bloody cranesbill), 15in. (38cm), red/purple flowers in summer, Europe.

Helianthemum chamaecistus (common rock rose), 3–24in. (7–61cm), yellow flowers in summer, Europe.

Potentilla verna, 3–9in. (7–23cm), yellow flowers in spring, Europe.

Saxifraga aizoon syn. *S. paniculata* (livelong saxifrage), 1in. (2cm), white flowers in summer, Europe.

Seline acaulis, (moss campion), 1–4in. (2–10cm), pink flowers in summer, Europe and N. America.

Sedum acre (yellow stonecrop) 1–6in. (2–15cm), yellow flowers in summer, America and Europe.

Sedum album (white stonecrop), 2–9in. (5–23cm), white flowers in summer, Europe.

Sedum anglicum (English stonecrop), 2in. (5cm), white flowers in summer, Europe.

Sedum pulchellum, 4–15in. (10–38cm), pink flowers in summer, N. America.

Sedum ternatum, 4–6in. (10–15cm), white flowers in summer, N. America.

Sempervivum tectorum, (houseleek), 9in. (23cm), purple flowers in summer, Europe.

Umbilicus rupestris (wall pennywort), 4in. (10cm), Europe.

Perennial flowering plants for scree soils

Adonis vernalis (yellow pheasant's eye), 6–15in. (15–38cm), Europe and N. America.

Alchemilla alpina (alpine lady's mantle), 6in. (15cm), green flowers in summer, Europe.

Dryas octopetala (mountain avens), spread 18in. (46cm), 2in. (5cm) white flowers in spring, Europe.

Dryas Drummondii, 3in. (8cm), yellow flowers in summer, N. America.

Geranium robertianum (herb robert), 4–20in. (10–51cm), pink flowers in summer, Europe and N. America.

Geranium sanguineum (bloody cranesbill), 15in. (38cm), red/purple flowers in summer, Europe.

Helianthemum chamaecistus (common rock rose), 3–24in. (7–61cm), yellow flowers in summer, Europe.

Meconopsis cambrica (yellow Welsh poppy), 8in. (20cm), yellow flowers in summer, Europe.

Oxalis acetosella (wood sorrel), 2in. (5cm), white flowers in spring, Europe and N. America.

Oxalis oregana, 3–8in. (7–20cm), red flowers in spring, N. America.

Saxifraga oppositifolia (purple saxifrage), 2in. (5cm), pink flowers in spring, Europe.

Sedum rosea (roseroot), 12in. (30cm), yellow flowers in summer, Europe and N. America.

Silene acaulus (moss campion), 3in. (7cm), rose pink flowers in spring, Europe and N. America.

Woodland areas where there is deep or dappled shade offer the widest scope for the planting of native species. A neutral-to-slightly-acid soil, composed of sandy loam and rotted leafmould, will suit most woodland flowering plants and complement the ferns of *Athyrium*, *Blechnum*, *Dryopteris* and *Woodwardia* genera.

Perennial woodland flowering plants

Adoxa moschatellina (moschatel), 2in. (5cm), green flowers in spring, Europe.

Anemone nemorosa (wood anemone), 6in. (15cm), white flowers in spring, Europe.

Arum maculatum (lords and ladies), 6in. (15cm), yellow flowers in spring, red berries in summer, Europe.

Aquilegia vulgaris, (columbine), 12–24in. (30–60cm), mauve flowers in summer, Europe and N. America.

Chrysosplenium oppositifolium (golden saxifrage), 3in. (7in), yellow flowers in summer, Europe.

Chrysosplenium americanum, 3in. (7cm), yellow flowers in summer, N. America.

Campanula rotundifolia (harebell), 6in. (15cm), blue flowers in summer, Europe.

Campanula Scouleri, 12in. (30cm), blue flowers in summer, N. America.

Convallaria majalis (lily of the valley), 6in. (15 cm), white flowers in spring, Europe.

Digitalis purpurea (foxglove), 36in. (90cm), purple flowers in summer, Europe.

Endymion non-scriptus (blubell), 12in. (30cm), blue flowers in spring, Europe.

Filipendula ulmaria (meadowsweet), 5ft. (1.5m), white flowers in summer, Europe.

Fragaria vesca (wild strawberry), 6in. (15cm), white flowers in spring and summer, Europe and N. America.

Guem urbanum (wood avens), 12in. (30cm), yellow flowers in summer, Europe and N. America.

Lonicera periclymenum (honeysuckle), 10–20ft. (3–6m), pink flowers in summer, Europe and N. America.

Melandrium rubrum (red campion), 36in. (90cm), red flowers in summer, Europe.

Mercurialis perennis (dog's mercury), 3in. (7cm), green flowers in spring, Europe.

Oxalis acetosella, 3in. (8cm), white flowers in spring, Europe and N. America.

Primula veris, (cowslip), 6in. (15 cm), yellow flowers in spring, Europe.

Primula vulgaris (primrose), 6in. (15 cm), yellow flowers in spring, Europe.

Ranunculus ficaria (lesser celandine), 3–10in. (7–25cm), yellow flowers in spring, Europe.

Viola pedata, 2–6in. (5–15cm), lilac flowers in spring, N. America.

Viola odorata (sweet violet), 6in. (15 cm), blue flowers in spring, Europe.

Viola riviniana (common dog-violet), 6in. (15cm), violet flowers in spring, Europe.

The damp or boggy soils alongside streams and pools can be host to a rich variety of wild flowers which, like *Oreopteris limbosperma* and *Onoclea sensibilis*, and the genera *Adiantum*, *Blechnum*, *Dryopteris*, *Osmunda*, and *Matteuccia*, will relish a peaty, acidic soil. If the existing soil is particularly heavy, a good amount of gritty leafmould should be introduced in the planting area. Light, chalky soils will need additional loam and leafmould in equal amounts.

Flowering plants for wetland and poolside planting

Caltha leptosepala, 12in. (30cm), white flowers in spring, N. America.

Caltha palustris (marsh marigold), 12in. (30cm), yellow flowers in spring, Europe.

Cardamine pratensis (lady's smock), 12–18in. (30–45cm), white flowers in summer, Europe.

Drosera rotundifolia (sun dew), 4in. (10cm), white flowers in summer, Europe.

Epipactis gigantea, 36in. (90cm), green flowers in summer, N. America.

Epipactis palustris (marsh helleborine), 12in. (30cm), purple flowers in summer, Europe.

Filipendula ulmaria (meadowsweet), 36in. (90cm), white flowers in summer, Europe.

Fritillaria meleagris (fritillary), 12in. (30cm), purple, yellow and white flowers in spring, Europe.

Fritillaria pudica, 6in. (15cm), yellow flowers in spring, N. America.

Hammarbya paludosa (bog orchid), 2in. (5cm), greenish-brown flowers in summer, Europe.

Lychnis flos-cuculi (ragged robin), 12in. (30cm), rose flowers in summer, Europe.

Lysimachia thyrsiflora, 36in. (90cm), yellow flowers in summer, Europe and N. America.

Lysimachia vulgaris (yellow loosestrife), 36in. (90cm), yellow flowers in summer, Europe.

Myosotis palustris (water forget-me-not), 6in. (15cm), blue flowers in spring, Europe.

Parnassia caroliniana, 6in. (15cm), white flowers in summer, N. America.

Parnassia palustris (grass of Parnassus), 6in. (15cm), white and green flowers in summer, Europe.

Senecio glabellus, 24in. (60cm), yellow flowers in spring, N. America.

Viola palustris (marsh violet), 4in. (10cm), pale lilac to white flowers in spring, Europe.

Many wild plants can be adapted for cultivation within a pond. Even small ponds can be host to a variety of wild flowering plants. For ease of maintenance, plants should be potted in open-weave plastic pots containing an equal mix of heavy loam and leafmould. Plant in early spring.

Aquatic flowering species within the pond

Eupatorium cannabinum (hemp agrimony), 24–48in. (60–120cm), reddish-purple flowers in summer, Europe.

Equisetum fluviatile (water horsetail), 24in. (60cm), Europe and N. America.

Hottonia palustris (water violet), 8in. (20cm), lilac flowers in summer, Europe.

Iris pseudacorus (yellow flag iris), 36in. (90cm), yellow flowers in spring, Europe.

Isoetes lacustris (common quill-wort), quill-like leaves, Europe and N. America.

Lythrum alatum, 24–48in. (60–120cm), purple flowers in summer, N. America.

Lythrum salicaria, (purple loosestrife), 36–48in. (60–120cm), purple flowers in summer, Europe.

Menyanthes trifoliata (buckbean), pinkish flowers in summer, Europe.

Nuphar advena, yellow flowers in spring and summer, N. America.

Nuphar lutea (yellow waterlily), yellow flowers in summer, Europe.

Nymphaea alba (white waterlily), white flowers in summer, Europe.

Nymphaea odorata, white flowers in summer, N. America.
Veronica beccabunga (brooklime), 9in. (22cm), blue flowers in summer, Europe.

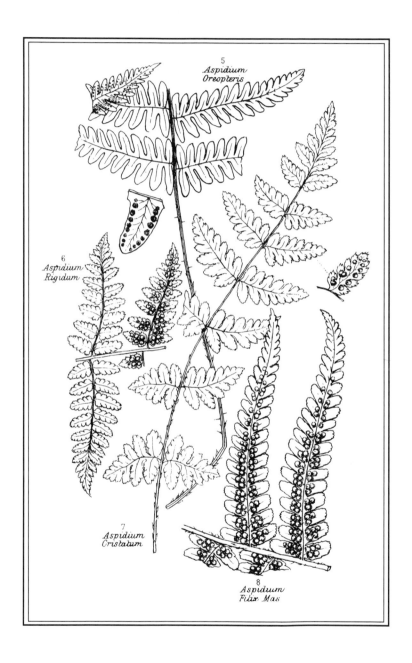

7

PREPARATION FOR INDOOR FERN CULTIVATION

Fern cultivation need not be confined to the garden. Indoor gardening with ferns, regardless of scale, affords the opportunity to appreciate at close quarters, and to create some dramatic effects with a plant group of startlingly diverse architectural forms. As equally varied as the configuration of the ferns is the variety of indoor settings which can be host to this distinctive plant group. From the lavishly equipped tropical greenhouse to the humble window sill of a centrally heated room, the range of conditions prevailing indoors can be matched by a selection of ferns which will prosper in chosen locations.

A major distinction of ferns as indoor plants lies in the luxuriance and longevity of their foliage. Most ferns, both tender and hardy, will remain evergreen in indoor cultivation, allowing a year-long display. Even those species which drop their fronds during their dormant season, such as the *Davallia*, retain our interest with the bizarre configuration of their furry rhizomes, which sprawl over pots or encircle baskets like hoary claws.

For indoor cultivation in all but the warmest climates, selection can be made from hardy, semi-hardy, semi-tender and tender species. The hardy species of ferns originate from temperate regions, where cool summers and cold winters prevail. These ferns need low cool-season temperatures, and are unsuitable for semi-tropical climates. Indoors, they are accommodating plants, adapting to a range of conditions from unheated rooms to the cool greenhouse. Hardy ferns, while not attaining the luxuriance of many tropical species, will provide, with the minimum of adaptation of locations and the minimum attention, splendid focal points in domestic interiors. Most hardy species will withstand more easily than exotic species fluctuations of temperature and humidity. Semi-hardy species will withstand short periods of frost, though they prefer minimum cool-season temperatures of 40°F (5°C). Many originate from Japan and, like the hardy species, they have a more robust constitution than tender species, making them an admirable choice for unheated greenhouses and difficult interiors.

Semi-tender ferns originate in warm and semi-tropical regions. They require minimum night temperatures of 50°F (10°C), with day temperatures some ten degrees higher. During the warmest months, the daytime temperature should be 70–80°F (21–27°C). The majority need humidity levels of

50–60 per cent for satisfactory growth. These conditions can be offered in the cool greenhouse, the conservatory and, with some modification, domestic interiors.

Tender ferns, native to the tropics, are more demanding of year-round warmth and high humidity. This group needs to be given minimum night temperatures of 60°F (16°C), with day temperatures some 10° higher. In the warmest months, the daytime temperature should be 70–80°F (21–27°C). Humidity levels of 60 per cent should be maintained during the growing season, and reduced to 50 per cent in the dormant season.

This broad classification masks the flexibility particular ferns possess in adapting to local conditions indoors. Ferns with robust, coarse fronds, such as *Blechnum* species, will accept less than ideal conditions more easily than will those ferns with thin or finely-formed fronds such as *Adiantum* species, which need an environment closely matching conditions in their native habitats.

The selection of species for indoor cultivation will depend in large measure upon the environment that can be offered. Therefore, it is important to evaluate the prevailing conditions and to determine to what extent, if any, those conditions can be adapted, with the minimum of inconvenience, to fern cultivation. Warmth, humidity and light levels will be the main factors which will influence the species of fern grown in particular settings.

For those gardeners who can achieve indoors optimum cultivation conditions, offered by the warm greenhouse or conservatory, an enormous range of species is available. The dilemma will be in selecting from such a diverse and interesting range. However, almost all indoor locations can provide some degree of control over temperature and humidity. With some ingenuity, even the unpromising conditions created by domestic central heating, where humidity is rarely above 30 per cent, can be offset sufficiently to allow many ferns to prosper indoors.

GROWING FERNS IN THE GREENHOUSE

The warm house, where the minimum night temperature is 60–65°F (15–18°C) and where a humidity level of 60 per cent can be maintained, offers ideal conditions for the cultivation of tropical and sub-tropical ferns. In summer, day temperatures may be expected to reach 75°F (24°C). Clearly such levels of temperature and humidity are suited to the greenhouse rather than the conservatory, and in practice only gardeners in warm climates will achieve these levels if heating costs are not to prove ruinous.

For greenhouse gardeners in northern parts of Europe and the USA, the cool house may be a more practicable alternative. Offering a minimum night temperature of 50–55°F (10–13°C), with day temperatures some ten degrees higher, will reduce the range of tender ferns that can be grown. However, the selection of ferns available for the cool greenhouse is still considerable. One valuable consolation of the cool house is that hardy species will also find the conditions favourable. When grown in the warm house or outdoors in sub-tropical climates the hardy ferns of temperate areas rarely succeed, as they require low temperatures in their dormant season. The unheated house, in temperate climates, will provide a good location for hardy and semi-hardy ferns. If good ventilation is provided and the plants kept barely moist during the coldest months, the unheated house can give adequate protection to semi-hardy ferns. The main enemy of these ferns in the cold months is not the occasional sharp frost, but rather permanently damp soil around the roots. Roller blinds, particularly if fitted to the exterior of the house, will help reduce heat loss. These should be drawn to cover the glass at dusk and be removed in the morning. Semi-hardy ferns over-wintered in cold frames can be given some frost-protection by covering the glass on the coldest night with hessian (burlap), sacks or straw.

Adapting conditions under glass for ferns

Ideally, a greenhouse devoted to ferns should be placed in a shaded part of the garden. A north-facing wall would be an ideal site for the construction of a lean-to fernery. Such a situation would give the benefit of sufficiently good light levels without the danger of direct sunlight scorching the fronds of the ferns. Where an exterior house wall forms part of the greenhouse it will also provide some supplementary warmth, radiated from domestic heating. A further advantage of the lean-to house is the option of extending into the greenhouse, with minimum inconvenience, the domestic central heating system to generate the primary source of heating.

A free-standing greenhouse should be sited in a shady part of the garden. A location in the shade cast by deciduous trees would be particularly favourable, the canopy of leaf cover protecting the house from strong summer sun and offering, at the fall of leaf, access to weaker winter light.

Any greenhouse, however, regardless of its location in the garden, can be adapted to provide suitable conditions for ferns. Where an existing green-house is being converted for fern cultivation it is likely to be sited to receive optimum sunlight. In these conditions some form of shading will have to be provided. Whitewashing the glass panes, an inexpensive option, will reduce sunlight levels but lacks sufficient flexibility to cater for the variable weather conditions that can be expected during the ferns' extended growing season. Roller blinds, constructed of slim wood slats or close-weave fabric, offer the most adaptable form of shading, permitting the gardener to vary the shading inside the house to suit the seasonal changes in light. For simplicity of operation and ease of maintenance they are best fitted to the exterior of the house. During spring and summer the shading will protect the ferns from wide fluctuations of temperature and direct sunlight scorching the fronds of the more delicate species. In autumn and winter, when light levels are reduced, the shading can be removed.

The house should also have sufficient ventilation to allow free circulation of air around the plants. If vents are placed at either end of small greenhouses this will allow the through-passage of air. Larger greenhouses will need ventilation at points throughout the span. Electric fans can help to ensure good ventilation during very warm periods, when there is little air movement. In practice, ventilators should be open in all but blustery conditions. Free passage of air around the plants will promote healthy growth and minimize disease and pest problems. Greenhouses which have been used for other plants, or which have been unused for some time, should be thoroughly cleaned. Sterilization of the glass, interior framework and staging is strongly recommended. In addition, any existing compost and soil in the greenhouse should be replaced, where practicable, by fresh, sterilized material. The effort involved in these procedures should ensure that the ferns subsequently introduced have the best possible chance of remaining pest and disease free.

The fern house will need large quantities of water throughout the year. A particularly useful item for such a house is a water storage tank linked to domestic guttering and overflows. Although many ferns will tolerate tapwater, the mineral salts from this accumulate in pots and in the soil, causing discoloration of the fronds of some ferns. It is therefore a good policy to use rainwater for all ferns. For convenience, if space permits, the water tank should be sited inside the greenhouse. In addition to regular watering of the plants, an overall humidity level of 50–60 per cent will need to be maintained throughout the house from spring to autumn. By far the most satisfactory solution to the problem of achieving the necessary levels of humidity is to ensure that benches and floors are hosed down regularly. During the hottest months of the year this will need to be done on a daily basis.

Thought should be given to the layout of the greenhouse in order to maximize the space available and to create suitable environments for a range of ferns. This may not be a consideration for the gardener who merely wishes to over-winter tender species intended for container display in the open garden during the warmer months. In this case, little maintenance will be required beyond ensuring that over-wintered plants are kept barely moist, and that decayed fronds are removed. In the dormant season a lower humidity level, in the order of 40–50 per cent, will not be detrimental to over-wintering ferns. In spring, when the new growth starts, the humidity level should be increased to 50–60 per cent. Pot-grown plants should be repotted with fresh compost, composed of two parts sterilized loam and two parts well-rotted leafmould to one part sharp sand. Alternatively, if leafmould is not available substitute with peat or coconut fibre. When repotting, choose a pot one size larger than the previous one. Ferns grown in baskets and rafts need not be disturbed unless they have obviously outgrown the container, but will benefit from a liquid feed of slow-release fertilizer at half the recommended strength. Before being placed out in the garden in late spring, the plants should be hardened off in a cold frame for a week or so. Acclimatization to outdoor conditions can be achieved by removing the covering of the frame for increasingly long periods during this time.

Where ferns are to be housed throughout the year, it is worth adapting the interior of the basic greenhouse to enhance conditions for fern growing. The shallow staging which is a feature of most small greenhouses makes an unsatisfactory area for housing ferns. Shallow stagings can be built up, ideally to a height of six inches, by attaching planks of wood around the existing staging, secured at points along their length. The area thus built up can be filled with a mix of grit or fine gravel. This will create a well-drained bed into which pots can be plunged. If peat or well-rotted leafmould is added, in porportions of six parts grit to one each of peat or leafmould, a good medium is created for the chance propagation of the ripened spores from established plants. These deep benches will allow pots to be plunged into a good depth of material, reducing the plants' moisture loss and ensuring a stable, cool temperature at the roots. Where shallow pans are used instead of pots, they can be fully immersed in the plunge material. This will allow a more harmonious display than will be possible where tall pots compete with the plants for attention.

Although the cultivation of ferns in pots offers the flexibility to change the layout of the display, an area of the staging might be assigned to the establishing of a permanent fern garden, using small species. Suitably contoured with lightweight rocks such as tufa, a miniature landscape can be designed which will reflect natural growing conditions. The smaller ferns of rocky habitats are the most suited to this type of open-bench cultivation. Good drainage is essential. The bed will need at least an inch of coarse grit or gravel as drainage. The growing medium should consist of a mix of equal parts grit, sterilized loam and well-rotted leafmould. Ferns requiring a more moist soil will impose too heavy a burden of weight on staging. They are best grown in beds constructed at ground level.

FERNS IN THE CONSERVATORY

The conservatory combines the beauty and charm of the garden with the comfort and convenience of the hearth. It should be kept in mind, however, that this type of gardening represents a compromise between the optimum cultivation needs of plants and the convenience of the owner. A well-informed choice of fern subjects, and well-planned conservatory layout, will do much to resolve these contradictory demands.

The main distinction between the cool greenhouse and the conservatory is the difficulty in ensuring sufficient levels of humidity in the latter structure. Clearly, levels of 50 per cent humidity, achieved in the greenhouse by hosing down floors, will be impractical where the conservatory is an integral part of the living area. In this situation the conservatory gardener can choose the option of growing those species which will happily tolerate lower levels of humidity. Alternatively, some simple devices can be employed which will improve levels of humidity around the plants. For those gardeners who choose the former option many species are available which will tolerate low humidity levels. The slightly more demanding option, although entailing more trouble and closer monitoring of plants, will allow the more luxuriant and delicately-formed species to prosper in the conservatory.

Generally constructed to receive maximum sunlight, conservatories may have considerable fluctuations in temperature between day and night. Adequate heating and ventilation should be employed to ensure a minimum temperature of 50°F (10°C) and, in the warmest season, a maximum day temperature of 75°F (24°C). Where heating is provided by radiators, it may be prudent to enlist fans to distribute the warm air evenly throughout the room. This will avoid pockets of warmed air being trapped near the radiators and relatively cool air lingering at those points furthest from the source of heat. Simple humidifiers can be constructed by suspending shallow troughs of water from radiators or from convenient points along the wall. Combined with an electric fan, such simple devices can significantly improve humidity levels.

Roller blinds, constructed from translucent material, will mitigate the most extreme variations in light and temperature. The degree of light transmitted by the fabric will depend upon the location. In the sunny, southern states of the USA a 50 per cent absorption rate may be required. In more northern latitudes a 30 per cent absorption rate is suitable. During winter, blinds should be drawn in the evening to reduce heat-loss through the glazing. In the morning the blinds should be raised. From late spring until early autumn blinds will be needed during the day to protect the ferns from full sun.

The provision and maintenance of adequate ventilation throughout the conservatory is an important factor in the creation of a suitable environment for ferns. Where conservatories are sited in south-facing locations, temperatures under the glass can rise dramatically during long sunny days. From spring until autumn good ventilation should be provided. In winter, constant ventilation during the day will prove impractical in rooms which function both as living areas and gardens. During this period, electric fans will be sufficient to provide a reasonable degree of ventilation.

FERNS AS HOUSEPLANTS AND IN WINDOW BOXES

The ferns' decline in popularity, happily now being reversed, can be traced to their reputation as 'difficult' house plants. Certainly, some species can be demanding in their needs for high levels of humidity, generally unattainable in domestic interiors. The various *Adiantum* species, darlings of the floristry trade and the impulse purchases of many novice gardeners seeking an attractive potted plant, require more care in cultivation than most indoor plants. Unless these species are given improved levels of humidity the fronds will become dessicated and shrivel.

Indoors, the main enemy of most ferns will prove to be the dry air created by central heating. As well as increasing the plant's water-loss through evaporation, central heating also reduces the humidity of the air around the plant, often producing humidity levels as low as 30 per cent. Such low levels can be mitigated by improving the humidity in the immediate vicinity of the plant. This can be achieved by frequent and regular misting of the foliage. This is a very efficient method where only a few ferns are grown. Where a larger number of ferns are grown, misting individual plants can become tedious and time consuming. Fortunately, there are other strategies which can be employed to provide a constant enhancement of humidity. The simple expedient of placing pots on dishes filled with pebbles and water will increase local humidity around the plant. The reservoir of water should be replenished at frequent intervals, making sure not to over-fill. At no time should the water in the dish be in contact with the base of the pot. The constant evaporation of water will provide an envelope of humid air around the plant. A further solution to the problems created by central heating is to establish plants in groups. This will reduce the burden of watering, and with the plants clustered together it will help to increase the overall humidity around individual plants. Alternatively, individual potted ferns or groups of plants can be plunged into larger containers filled with damp peat. This method has the added attraction of providing the ferns with stable temperatures at their roots as well as creating a continual source of damp air around the fronds. The peat-filled container should be replenished with water at frequent intervals to ensure maximum humidity.

Most ferns cultivated indoors require the indirect light created by diffused sunlight. Direct exposure to sun in a south-facing window will generally be harmful to most ferns, leading to the dessication of the fronds of finely formed species. Where ferns are used in a window display, a north-facing aspect should be chosen. Ferns will tolerate remarkably lower levels of light than most flowering plants, although very gloomy conditions will not inspire satisfactory growth. Experimentation with various locations within the house, combined with careful observation of growth, will inform the tolerance of particular plants. (Chapter 10 offers guidance on species' requirements which can be used to initiate experimentation.)

The use of supplementary lighting will allow many ferns to prosper in those very gloomy interiors which otherwise would not support plant life. Domestic light bulbs should be avoided as they produce too much heat, which will inevitably scorch fronds. Specialist growing lamps, used by professional growers, will produce optimum lighting conditions for growing ferns. However, in domestic interiors aesthetic considerations may make the use of these undesirable. Fluorescent lamps offer the best compromise, combining cool operating temperatures with relative unobtrusiveness. Place the lights, preferably cool white, in pairs from 12–24 inches above the tallest fronds. Some experimentation may be needed to determine the length of time the supplementary lighting should be provided during the day. In dim interiors it may be required for 8–12 hours.

GROWING FERNS IN POTS AND CONTAINERS

Enhancing local humidity

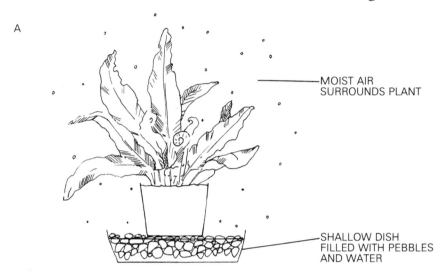

A

MOIST AIR
SURROUNDS PLANT

SHALLOW DISH
FILLED WITH PEBBLES
AND WATER

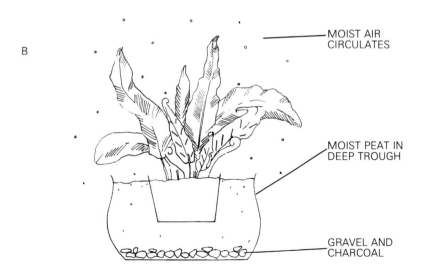

MOIST AIR
CIRCULATES

B

MOIST PEAT IN
DEEP TROUGH

GRAVEL AND
CHARCOAL

Most ferns grown indoors are cultivated in pots. To ensure success throughout their potentially lengthy life span indoors, care is needed to match the size of the plant with compatible soil conditions and size of pot. Over a period of years, as the plant matures and develops its root system, it will require a succession of larger pots and the renewal of the soil. Young ferns need to be repotted each year, preferably in early spring and just prior to the emergence of new fronds. Mature ferns which have graduated to large pots need not be repotted, but will benefit from the removal of some of the exhausted soil and its replenishment with fresh material. Alternatively, the fern can be removed from the pot, the roots shaken free of soil and the plant repotted in fresh soil. Any obviously dead parts of the rootstock should be carefully cut away before repotting in the original pot.

Pots should be just large enough to contain the roots. The shallow root system of ferns makes shallow pans a good alternative to pots. Over-potting, placing the plant in a pot too large for its root system, will result in a sour soil and weak growth. The root system will be unable to take up the available water and consequently the soil will become waterlogged and impervious to the air required by the roots.

Adequate drainage and a good soil mix will ensure that plants have a good growing medium. The bottom third of the pot should be filled with crushed brick, crocks or stones. The planting mix for most species should consist of one part commercial compost or sterilized loam, one part sharp sand and two parts well-rotted leafmould. A small amount of granulated charcoal added to the soil will keep the soil sweet. For those ferns which thrive on an alkaline soil, one part limestone chippings should be added to the basic mixture. If clay pots are used they should be soaked overnight before use to ensure that the clay does not absorb the water from the soil, causing the newly potted plant to wilt.

For indoor cultivation, where there is a greater danger of ferns suffering drought through the inadvertent neglect of watering routines, plastic pots are the most practical choice for small and medium-sized ferns. These will dry out less quickly than clay pots. Large 'accent' plants can be planted in clay pots or, alternatively, plastic pots can be disguised by being plunged in raffia baskets.

Watering

Initially, careful vigilance will need to be maintained to ensure that the plants, whether in beds, pots or other containers, receive sufficient moisture. Frequent, superficial watering is harmful to most plants and to ferns in particular. Apart from aquatic and semi-aquatic species, pot-grown ferns should be allowed to become almost dry before the next thorough watering. The peculiarities of individual areas, whether in the greenhouse, the conservatory or living areas, will dictate the frequency of watering. The degree of shade cover, ventilation, prevailing climate and humidity level will affect the plants' water absorption. During the growing period, from spring through to autumn, ferns will require frequent watering. This is particularly the case with pot-grown specimens cultivated under glass or indoors. It is well worth examining plants each day, keeping a written or mental note of the moisture loss of individual plants. Several methods can be used to determine the amount of moisture in the soil. Surface dryness is not a reliable guide. It is better to examine the soil an inch or more below the surface. If it is still moist there, watering is not yet required. With experience and practice, the weight of pots will be a guide to the dryness of the soil, a light pot indicating that watering may be required. Many people advocate tapping clay pots as a reliable guide to watering. A pot which gives off a dull sound when tapped sharply has sufficient moisture. A hollow sound will signify the need for watering.

With such observations it is possible to build up a picture of the moisture requirements of particular plants, which can be used to inform a reliable watering regime. Variations will need to be made in such a regime for fluctuations in the weather. It is often overlooked that air conditions can have a significant effect on plants grown under glass. Warm, drying winds or humid, still conditions will affect humidity and moisture levels almost as much as periods of prolonged sunshine or overcast skies.

During their dormant period, in winter, the plants should be kept barely moist. At this time pot-grown ferns will require the minimum of moisture, and reduced levels of humidity. High humidity, above 50 per cent, and wet, soggy soil will produce the stagnant conditions which could lead to fungal diseases. Maintenance can be confined to removing decayed fronds and ensuring that the house is well ventilated. Stunted, weak growth, sometimes produced at this time by ferns which have been given over-moist conditions around the roots, should be cut back. In spring, when growth recommences, plants may be given a liquid feed of slow-release fertilizer at half the recommended strength.

Pests and diseases

Generally, ferns grown indoors are less prone to attack by insects than many other types of plants. Where ferns are grown alongside other plants in the greenhouse they may be invaded by whitefly, a tiny moth-like creature which secretes a sticky honeydew. Ferns should be washed down with a mild detergent solution to remove the infestation. A chemical treatment should be given to the plants which harbour the pest. Avoid treating ferns with such chemicals.

Attacks by mealy bugs are signalled by the appearance of white fluffy insects on the rachis and fronds. Infected fronds will show signs of wilting and yellowing. Spray or wash the affected parts with a mild detergent solution, or remove and destroy affected fronds.

Scale insects, appearing as small brown discs on the frond or rachis, suck the sap of the plant, leaving a sticky honeydew secretion. *Asplenium nidus* (bird's nest fern) is particularly prone to attack by this pest. In the case of severe infestation, the whole plant should be removed and burned.

Red spider mite is a common pest of ferns and other plants which are cultivated in settings which are insufficiently humid. The pest is minute and difficult to spot. Signs of infestation are blotches on the fronds, wispy webbing on frond bases, and lack of plant growth. This pest can be controlled by improving humidity around the plant, by frequent, regular spraying, or by resting pots on a dish filled with water and gravel.

The small, white grubs of the vine weevil (*Otiorhynchus sulcatus*) feed on the roots of all pot-grown plants. If the adult beetle is seen on fronds or the surface of the soil, or if infestation is suspected, remove the plants from the pot and discard the soil. Wash the roots carefully to remove any grubs and repot in uncontaminated compost. Douse all soils with gamma-HCH insecticide. Sterilise the staging and remove traces of plant debris within the house which might harbour the adult weevils.

Mould and fungus may develop if good hygiene and adequate ventilation are not maintained. Wilted or damaged fronds should be removed throughout the year. Look out for mildew secretions on fronds, which if unchecked can quickly be host to fungal disease. A combination of over-watering and under-ventilation is the main cause of disease in ferns. In their dormant season ferns, with the exception of aquatic species, need to be kept barely moist. Allow a free passage of air around the plants and ensure that ferns planted in groups are not over-crowded.

8
GROWING FERNS INDOORS

Indoor fern cultivation has a substantial tradition. With the exception of culinary plants, ferns were among the first exotics to be grown indoors in Europe. Today, the resurgence of interest in ferns is indicated by the extent to which these most graceful and charming plants are used to enhance commercial and domestic interiors.

In Europe during the late eighteenth century, before interest in native species was stimulated, fern cultivation was largely confined to those tender species brought back to Europe from exotic locations on the wave of expedition and colonization that happened then. These ferns were cultivated in the stove houses of country estates and botanic gardens. Such stove houses, capable of sustaining minimum night temperatures of at least 70°F (21°C), were a rare luxury confined to the botanically curious, who had both the leisure and wealth to indulge in this demanding pursuit.

In contrast to present-day plant houses, with their expanses of clear glazing and efficient heating and ventilation, eighteenth-century stoves offered plants a poor environment. The small panes of glass, hand crafted from blown glass, were inefficient transmitters of light, absorbing up to 70 per cent of the available illumination. The flimsy panes occupied a small percentage of the building, which was composed of a stout framework of wooden beams or stonework. Heat was generated either from fermenting dung pits within the stove house or from flues channelled through the building. Despite some experimentation – the London nurserymen Loggiges and Sons had some success with pressurized steam heating – the cultivation of exotics was a precarious venture. Low light levels, foul, dry air, and soot made these structures less than ideal for those plants whose native habitats were the humid forests or streambanks of the Americas or Asia.

The 1840s saw a rapid increase in the popularity of the indoor cultivation of ferns and flowering plants. The development was due, in part, to the advances in engineering and production methods brought about by industrialization. New techniques in metalworking permitted wrought iron to replace cumbersome wood and brick structures. This, together with the introduction of flat glass, allowed architects to create a transformation in stove houses. Developments in plumbing made possible the use of hot-water pipes as an efficient and clean method of heating. Throughout the remaining decades of the century, the horticultural press carried a flood of advertisements for these glass structures. Whether as free-standing greenhouses, designed to complement the garden, or as conservatories drawing the garden into the home, such objects became the status symbols of the affluent plant lover.

For the owners of greenhouses and conservatories, a wave of publications offered instruction in their furnishing, stocking and maintenance. A further incentive to indoor cultivation came from the exploits of plant hunters, who were returning to Europe with exotic species and descriptions of the fabulous flora of distant lands. These botanic explorers were elevated to the status of folk heroes and the fruits of their exploits, on display in the public gardens and private parks, were the subject of pilgrimage in an age committed to all things botanical.

The warm greenhouse, the counterpart to the Victorian stove house, offers a classical setting for the semi-tender and tender ferns. The scope of planting will be determined by the size of the planting area, but regardless of scale it is well worth creating a range of settings which can exploit, at least in part, the diversity of forms and habits the ferns exhibit. The lower temperatures of the cool greenhouse impose some limitations on the species that can be grown. They do not, however, restrict the variety of planting schemes that can be incorporated into these settings. Suggested plantings for the warm or cool greenhouse can be incorporated within conservatories where there are facilities for the efficient control of temperature, humidity and ventilation.

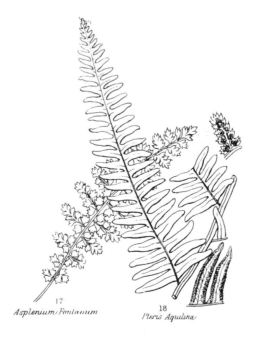

17
Asplenium Fontanum

18
Pteris Aquilina

In less favoured conservatories and within domestic interiors, the prevailing environment will place some limitations on the choice of species, in terms both of scale and the adaptability of particular species to less than ideal conditions. Temporary displays in difficult areas are possible if the ferns can be returned to more conducive environments, such as the greenhouse, for periodic recuperation. Alternatively, as suggested in the previous chapter, difficult sites can be modified locally to enhance growing conditions.

The unheated greenhouse will provide congenial conditions for hardy and semi-hardy species. The latter can be expected to survive occasional sharp frosts, provided they are not exposed to the prolonged periods of damp, cold conditions prevalent in the open garden. Good ventilation and a minimum amount of moisture around their roots will be sufficient to see them through all but the most severe winters.

In the following suggested schemes, the plants designated for cool greenhouses can also be grown in warm greenhouses. Those suggested for the unheated greenhouse can also be grown in the cool greenhouse.

TREE FERNS

In indoor areas which will accommodate them, the exotic grandeur of tree ferns will create spectacular 'accent' plants. Species are available which will suit the warm house or conservatory (60°F [16°C] minimum), cooler areas (50°F [10°C] minimum), and even unheated interiors (40°F [5°C] minimum). Tree ferns can be easily accommodated in pots until they reach large proportions. At that stage they should be transplanted into beds or borders indoors.

These ferns require a well-drained soil, composed of one part sterilized loam, two parts leafmould and one part sharp sand. Keep the soil moist during the growing period, but never soggy. Do not allow the soil to dry out at any time. In interiors with less than optimum levels of humidity (60 per cent) the trunk should be sprayed regularly. Further interest can be added to the tree ferns by training small epiphytic ferns such as *Pellaea rotundifolia* (button fern) on the bare trunk of larger specimens.

Tree ferns for indoor plantings

60°F (16°C)   *Alsophila australis, Cyathea arborea.*
50°F (10°C)   *Blechnum braziliense, B. gibbum, Cibotium glaucum, C. schiedei, Ctenitis Sloanei, Cyathea dealbata* syn. *Alsophilia tricolor, C. medullaris* syn. *Sphaeropteris medullaris, Dicksonia fibrosa, Diplazium esculentum, D. proliferum.*
40°F (5°C)   *Cyathea cooperi* syn. *Sphaeropteris cooperi, Dicksonia antarctica, D. fibrosa, D. squarrosa.*

The warm house 60°F (16°C)

Alsophila australis (Australian tree fern) makes an imposing 'accent' plant, with large, arching fronds emerging from the crown set in a tall trunk. Mature specimens, reaching beyond ten feet in height, with fronds of a similar size, are suitable only for the large warm greenhouse or conservatory. *Cyathea arborea* (West Indian tree fern), another arborescent species suitable only for the warm greenhouse or conservatory, will produce a multitude of smaller fronds cascading from the crown of a stout trunk.

The cool house 50°F (10°C)

Most tree ferns will tolerate the lower temperatures offered by the cool house. Where large specimens are desired *Cyathea dealbata* (silver tree fern), *C. medullaris* (black tree fern) and *Dicksonia fibrosa* should be chosen. More confined areas dictate the selection of more compact species such as *Blechnum braziliense*, *B. gibbum*, *Cibotium glaucum* (Hawaiian tree fern), *C. schiedei* (Mexican tree fern), *Diplazium esculentum* and *D. proliferum*. *Blechnum braziliense* and *B. gibbum* are extremely resilient, low-growing species. Their glossy, leathery fronds and their adaptability to rather dry conditions make them ideal for domestic interiors, where humidity is lower than most tree ferns demand. While not classed as tree ferns, both *Diplazium esculentum* and *D. proliferum* produce large, gracefully arching fronds from erect stems. *Diplazium proliferum* produces plantlets on the surface of its entire fronds. These can be detached and grown on to produce further specimens.

The frost-free house 40°F (5°C)

Where some protection from sharp frosts can be given, tree ferns can be grown in unheated interiors. *Dicksonia antarctica* (soft tree fern), perhaps the most frequently cultivated tree fern, with massive fronds 6–12ft. (1.8–3.6m) across, can be grown in these situations. Provide bright, indirect light and keep the soil moist. Other smaller species of *Dicksonia* relishing these conditions include *D. fibrosa* and *D. squarrosa*.

Many other larger species of fern make excellent 'accent' plants. Those ferns with a distinctive symmetry of frond architecture or with particularly striking frond forms should be chosen. In small areas, single specimens can be cultivated in pots filled with an equal mix of sterilized loam and leafmould. Larger areas are capable of producing dramatic effects by multiple planting of particular species in open beds. The large surface area of fronds, which is a feature of these ferns, entails the need for regular watering and high levels of humidity (50–60 per cent) to achieve optimum growth.

60°F (16°C) *Acrostichum aureum, Acrostichum daneaefolium* (swamp fern), *Cibotium Barometz* (Sythian lamb fern), *Microlepia speluncae, M. stringosa,*

50°F (10°C)   *Aglaomorpha coronans* syn. *A. pseudodrynaria*, *A. meyenianum* (bear's paw fern), *Asplenium nidus*, *Diplazium pynocarpon* (glade fern), *Hypolepis punctata*, *H. repense* (bramble fern), *Leptopteris superba* (Prince of Wales' feathers), *Nephrolepis acuminata*, *Polypodium coronans*, *P. crassifolium*.

40°F (5°C)   *Athyrium thelypteroides* (silver glade fern), *Dryopteris dilatata* (broad buckler), *D. filix-mas* var., *Dryopteris goldiana*, *Matteuccia pensylvanica*, *M. struthiopteris* (shuttlecock fern), *Osmunda cinnamomea (cinnamon fern)* *O. claytoniana* (interrupted fern), *Thelypteris palustris* (marsh fern), *Woodwardia radicans* (chain fern), *W. unigemmata* syn. *W. radicans unigemmata*, *W. virginica* (Virginia chain fern).

WATER FEATURE

A water feature, such as a small pool, affords the opportunity to introduce a large 'accent' plant alongside the pool margin. Although the following plants would prefer the boggy conditions of an open-bed planting alongside the pool, they can be grown in large pots containing a mix of equal parts sterilized loam and leafmould. Potted specimens can be placed within a second container, without drainage holes, and be partially submerged in the pool margin if required.

60°F (16°C)   *Acrostichum aureum* (leather fern), *Acrostichum daneaefolium*, *Diplazium pynocarpon*,

50°F (10°C)   *Leptopteris superba*, *Woodwardia* spp..

40°F (5°C)   *Matteuccia pensylvanica*, *Matteuccia struthiopteris*, *Onoclea sensibilis*, *Thelypteris noveboracensis*, *Thelypteris palustris*, *Woodwardia radicans* (chain fern), *Woodwardia virginica* (Virginia chain fern)

Small aquatic marginals

Pool margins offer ideal sites for those finely-formed species which relish moist conditions and high humidity. Species with creeping rhizomes are happier alongside the pool in open, free-draining sites. These will quickly colonize available space. In more cramped areas, ferns with erect rootstock, planted in shallow pans or in the soil, will provide a more diverse range of forms. *Selaginella*, a fern ally, *Adiantum*, *Blechnum* and *Nephrolepis* species will require minimum maintenance in this type of site. Plant in pots or open beds using a free-draining fern compost, composed of one part sterilized loam, one part sand, and one part leafmould.

60°F (16°C)   *Adiantum cultratum*, *A concinnum*, *Anemia rotundifolia*, *Blechnum orientale*, *Doryopteris ludens*, *Nephrolepis biserrata*, *Tectaria* spp..

50°F (10°C) *Adiantum cunninghamii, A. hispidulum, A. macrophyllum, Anemia phyllitidis, A. mexicana, Asplenium bulbiferum, A. nidus, Blechnum discolor, B. moorei.*

40°F (5°C) *Adiantum capillus-veneris, A. pedatum, Asplenium platyneuron, Athyrium* spp., *Blechnum fluviatile, B. penna-marina, B. nipponicum, B. spicant, Camptosorus rhizophyllus, Phyllitis scolopendrium* vars., *Woodsia* spp..

Aquatics

Amongst the most intriguing ferns are the aquatic species. Of all the fern species these are the least trouble to grow. They can be cultivated in a variety of aquatic situations ranging from small open dishes, filled with mud and rainwater, to large pools. Most of the floating ferns are fast-growing and will need to be cut back periodically when they become too invasive in large pools. *Equisetum* might be included in a pool setting. The variegated form, *E. variegatum*, grows 6–24in. (16–64cm), sending up clusters of reedy stems. *Equisetum* spp. are particularly invasive plants and must be grown in pots. Never plant in open ground as their roots, one established, are extremely difficult to eradicate. Plant in shallow pans using garden loam, and submerge the pans in the pool.

Two related genera of filmy ferns, *Hymenophyllum* and *Trichomanes*, are natural aquatic marginals, with delicate, translucent fronds ranging from 1–9in. (2–23cm) long. Increasingly rare in the wild, and now protected species, they are the most demanding ferns to grow. Native of streamside wet rocks in tropical and temperate areas, they require 100 per cent humidity and low, indirect light. In a poolside setting, both species can be cultivated on acid rocks almost completely submerged in water. Cover the rocks with sphagnum moss and attach the thread-like rhizomes to the moss with nylon fishing line. Alternatively a small log, floating freely in the pond, will make a naturalistic setting for these ferns. Again, cover the log with sphagnum moss and attach the fern's rhizomes to the moss, securing with nylon fishing line. In addition to filmy ferns, the log can be used as a planting site for some of the smaller epiphytes.

60°F (16°C) *Azolla caroliniana* (fairy moss), *Ceratopteris pteridoides, Ceratopteris thalictroides* (water sprite), *Marsilea fimbriata, Regnellidium diphyllum, Salvinea auriculata, Salvinea minima* (water spangles).

50°F (10°C) *Azolla caroliniana* (fairy moss), *Equisetum* spp., *Hymenophyllum tunbrigense* (Tunbridge filmy fern), *Hymenophyllum wilsonii* (Wilson's filmy fern), *Marsilea Drummondii, Marsilea hirsuta, Marsilea mutica, Marsilea quadrifolia* (nardoo plant/water clover), *Trichomanes* spp..

40°F (5°C) *Azolla filiculoides, Equisetum* spp., *Hymenophyllum demissum, Hymenophyllum tunbrigense* (Tunbridge filmy fern), *Hymeno-*

phyllum wilsonii (Wilson's filmy fern), *Marsilea Drummondii*, *Marsilea hirsuta, M. quadrifolia* (nardoo plant/water clover),

OPEN PLANTING

In greenhouses where the staging has been modified to allow deep beds of at least six inches in depth, permanent colonies of the most attractive small species can be planted out. Choose those with ascending or short creeping rhizomes, as these will remain fairly compact even over a number of years. The strength of the staging will dictate the scope of the planting. To keep the weight down to safe limits, small, rock-dwelling species are best in such locations. They will need a lesser volume of soil and less water than woodland or wetland species. The latter types are best cultivated at ground level in beds which have good drainage and a deep layer of fern compost composed of one part loam, one part sand and one part leafmould. Other areas under staging can provide an attractive location for those ferns which have a low-growing habit. These ferns, which generally have creeping rhizomes, can be left to spread at will.

Rather than a confusing mixture of ferns of differing habits and cultural requirements, it may prove more harmonious to order the planting within definable schemes. With a little forethought and planning, sections can be demarcated for calcareous and non-calcareous species, for species in a related genera or for species of similar geographic origin.

In conservatories and within the home, individual pots of ferns dotted around an area can present a cluttered appearance. More importantly, the chances of keeping the individual plants well-maintained are reduced. A fern left unwatered for too long will quickly wilt beyond recovery. For these reasons large-scale plantings of ferns are best achieved in tubs and troughs. To allow arrangements to be changed easily, plants can be potted individually and plunged into a trough filled with gravel or peat. Alternatively, plants can be removed from their pots and planted directly into containers. Good drainage will be provided by filling the bottom third of the container with coarse gravel, pebbles, small stones or broken brick. The planting medium for woodland and wetland ferns should be composed of one part sterilized loam, one part sharp sand or gravel and one part leafmould. Species native to rocky habitats will appreciate a grittier soil. Calcareous species should be given one part limestone chippings to three parts of the basic fern compost. Leave a gap of at least an inch between the level of soil and the rim of the container to facilitate watering.

When selecting plants for these areas keep acid-preferring and alkaline preferring species separate. Overcrowding of plants should be avoided as it will lead to stunted development and an unattractive display. Plants should be spaced to allow their fronds to develop without obstruction. For most species this will dictate a planting distance equal to their height.

Ferns for open planting or containers

Medium height 12–24in. (60–90cm)

60°F (16°C) *Doryopteris ludens, Doryopteris palmata, Drynaria quercifolia* (oak-leaf fern), *Drynaria ridigula, Pteris tremula* (table fern), *Tectaria cicutaria.*

50°F (10°C) *Adiantum* spp., *Asplenium nidus, Blechnum tabulare, Nephrolepis* spp., *Pityrogramma* spp..

40°F (5°C) *Adiantum pedatum, A. tenerum, Anemia adiantifolia, A. phyllitidis* (flowering fern), *Asplenium bulbiferum, A. platyneuron* (ebony spleenwort), *Athyrium filix-femina* vars. (lady fern), *A. goeringianum* 'Pictum' (Japanese painted fern), *A. thelypteroides* (silver glade fern), *Blechnum occidentale* (hammock fern), *B. spicant* (hard fern), *Ceterach aureum, Cyrtomium falcatum* (Japanese holly fern), *C. fortunei, Doodia aspera* (rasp fern), *D. maxima, D. media, Dryopteris* spp., *Onychium japonicum* (Japanese claw fern), *Pellaea atropurpurea* (purple rock brake), *Pellaea falcata, Pellaea viridis* (green rock brake), *Phyllitis scolopendrium* vars. (hart's tongue), *Polystichum acrostichoides* (Christmas fern), *Polystichum aculeatum* vars., *Polystichum adiantiforme, P. aristum, P. braunii, P. cystosterigia, P. lonchitis* (holly fern), *P. munitum, P. setiferum* vars., *Thelypteris hexagonoptera* (broad beech fern), *Thelypteris noveboracensis* (New York fern), *Todea barbara.*

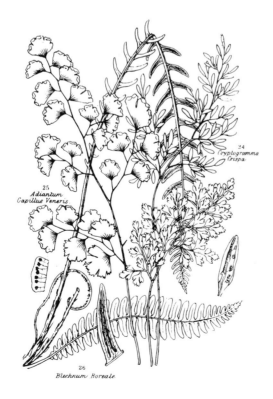

24
Cryptogramma Crispa

25
Adiantum Capillus Veneris

26
Blechnum Boreale

Small ferns under 12in. (30cm)

60°F (16°C) *Actinopteris australis, Adiantum macrophyllum, A. peruvianum, Anemia adiantifolia, Gymnopteris rufa, Humata* spp..

50°F (10°C) *Adiantum cunninghamii, A. incisum, Camptosorus rhizophyllus* (walking fern), *Ceterach dalhousiae, Doryopteris pedata, Drymoglossum piloselloides, Pteris* spp..

40°F (5°C) *Anogramma chaerophylla, A. leptophylla, Asplenium adiantum-nigrum* (black spleenwort), *A. platyneuron, A. ruta-muria* (wall spleenwort), *A. septentrionale* (forked spleenwort), *A. trichomanes* (maidenhair spleenwort), *A. viride* (green spleenwort), *Blechnum penna-marina, Ceterach officinarum, Cheilanthes lanosa, Cheilanthes marantae, Cheilanthes pteridioides, Cryptogramma crispa* (parsley fern), *Cystopteris fragilis* (brittle bladder fern), *Davallia mariesii* (ball fern), *Gymnocarpium dryopteris* (oak fern), *G. robertianum, Polystichum tsus-simense, Thelypteris phegopteris* (beech fern), *Woodsia alpina, Woodsia ilvensis, Woodsia obtusa, Woodsia scopulina.*

EPIPHYTIC FERNS

With a little ingenuity, the often-redundant space above the staging and walkways in the greenhouse can be given over to those ferns which, by growing habit or frond form, are least suited to bench or pot cultivation. Epiphytic ferns which naturally exploit walls, rocks and trees as habitats, using their creeping rhizomes to cling to moss or bark, are ideal subjects for this type of treatment.

A fallen sapling or tree branch which is free of disease, attached securely to the wall of a lean-to house or strung across the span of a free-standing house, can be used to grow several species of epiphytic fern. A branching or forked trunk will create a more pleasing effect than a uniform one and will offer a variety of planting heights. Any portion of the trunk which is to be inserted in soil must be first treated with preservative to prevent rot.

Bundles of sphagnum moss containing a little grit and leafmould at least an inch deep and of sufficient length to accommodate the rhizomes of the fern, should be attached at points along the trunk with thin wire or nylon fishing line. Remove the pot-grown epiphytes from their containers and free the rhizomes from the soil, if necessary flushing any traces of soil with running water. The rhizomes should be spread out onto the moss with the growing tips facing outward. Attach the rhizomes to the moss with wire. Cover the exposed rhizomes with an additional, thin layer of moss and secure the planting to the log with nylon fishing line. After the initial thorough watering, observation of the moss will indicate the necessary frequency of subsequent watering. While the moss remains deep green, the fern will have enough moisture. A yellowing of the moss will indicate that watering is needed.

Epiphytic ferns for cultivation

60°F (16°C)	*Davallia divaricata, Drymoglossum* spp., *Drynaria quercifolia, Elaphoglossum crinitum* (elephant's ear), *E. petiolatum, Humata* spp., *Leucostegia* spp., *Platycerium* spp., *Polypodium angustifolium, Polypodium aureum, P. coronans, P. crassifolium, Pyrrosia* spp., *Scyphularia pentaphylla, Vittaria elongata, V. scolopendrina.*
50°F (10°C)	*Davallia fejeensis, D. solida, Drynaria ridigula, Humata tyermannii, Phlebodium aureum, Platycerium bifurcatum, P. veitchii, Polypodium* spp., *P. lingua, Pyrrosia rupestris,*
40°F (5°C)	*Davallia canariensis* (hare's foot fern), *D. mariesii, D. pyxidata, D. trichomanoides, Polypodium australe, P. azoricum, P. interjectum, P. polypodioides, P. scouleri, P. vulgare.*

CLIMBING FERNS

Where branches or logs are introduced to provide planting sites for epiphytic species, these features can offer support for *Lygodium* species. These ferns will train themselves up suitable supports, reaching a height of 4–6ft. (1.2–1.8m.) in most greenhouses or conservatories. *Lygodium japonicum* (Japanese climbing fern) and *Lygodium palmatum* (Hartford fern) are the two most commonly cultivated. Both species require moist, acidic soil and a minimum temperature of 40°F (5°C). The deciduous *Lygodium japonicum* prefers bright indirect light. The evergreen *Lygodium palmatum*, a protected species, is difficult to cultivate successfully. It requires strongly acidic soil and deep shade.

60°F (16°C)	*Lygodium flexuosum, Lygodium microphyllum, L. scandens.*
50°F (10°C)	*Lygodium japonicum, Lygodium palmatum.*
40°F (5°C)	*Lygodium japonicum*

HANGING BASKETS

Rafts or baskets provide additional devices with which to maximize the use of space in the greenhouse or conservatory. Fern baskets can prove to be an ideal solution in busy domestic interiors, offering locations where plants can remain safe from the accidental knocks and spills to which shelf-mounted plants are often subjected. Although they will need more maintenance than floor-level containers, the appeal they confer on room interiors can make the extra effort worth while.

Suspended from the ceiling or attached to walls, this mode of cultivation is especially suited to ferns with erect rootstock, producing pronounced cascading fronds, such as *Adiantum* and *Nephrolepis*, whose arching fronds will quickly envelop the basket in a curtain of lacy greenery.

Ferns with erect rhizomes should be planted in the centre of a basket which has been lined with sphagnum moss and filled with a gritty fern compost, made of one part sterilized loam or commercial compost, one part coarse grit or gravel and one part leafmould. The crown of the fern should be just above the surface of the soil. Water the basket thoroughly and allow

Planting ascending rhizome-rooted ferns in rafts and baskets

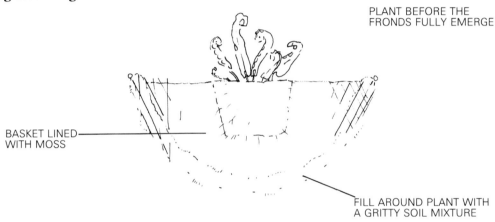

PLANT BEFORE THE
FRONDS FULLY EMERGE

BASKET LINED
WITH MOSS

FILL AROUND PLANT WITH
A GRITTY SOIL MIXTURE

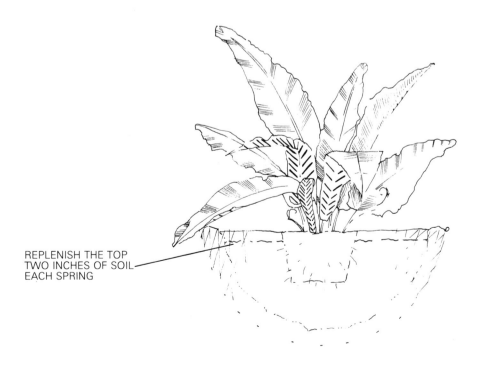

REPLENISH THE TOP
TWO INCHES OF SOIL
EACH SPRING

to drain before hanging it in the chosen site. As well as being misted frequently, baskets should be brought down and plunged in a basin of water whenever there is any suspicion that the moss lining is drying out. In indoor areas of low humidity, baskets will benefit from misting, preferably with rainwater, several times a week during the growing season.

Epiphytic ferns

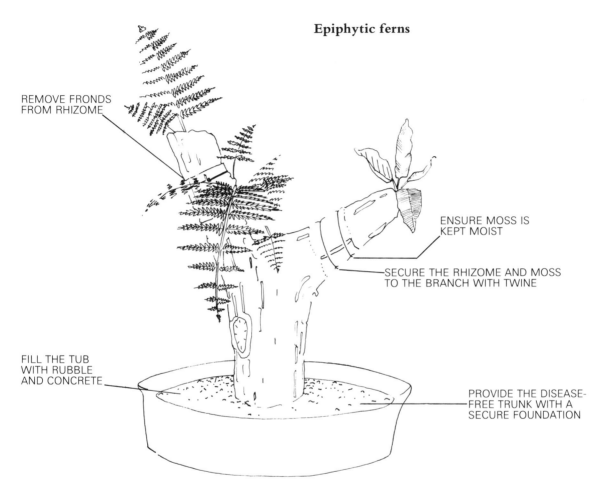

REMOVE FRONDS FROM RHIZOME

ENSURE MOSS IS KEPT MOIST

SECURE THE RHIZOME AND MOSS TO THE BRANCH WITH TWINE

FILL THE TUB WITH RUBBLE AND CONCRETE

PROVIDE THE DISEASE-FREE TRUNK WITH A SECURE FOUNDATION

The natural epiphytes, such as *Davallia* and *Polypodium* species, which have creeping rhizomes, are suitable ferns for planting in baskets and rafts. Baskets should be lined with an inch of sphagnum moss and filled with a very gritty fern compost, composed of two parts grit, one part sterilized loam or compost and one part leafmould. Insert rooted rhizomes, removed from mature specimens, around the circumference of the basket, with their roots embedded in the moss. Secure the rhizomes, if necessary, with wire. Further rhizomes are placed on the soil in the centre of the basket and covered with a layer of moss. Planting the basket is best undertaken in early spring when the buds of the new fronds are appearing on the surface of the rhizome. Water thoroughly after planting. Re-water when the moss shows signs of becoming dry.

Mounting a *Platycerium*

SEVER THE
PLANTLET FROM
THE PARENT

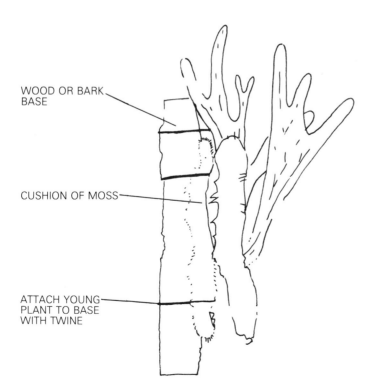

WOOD OR BARK
BASE

CUSHION OF MOSS

ATTACH YOUNG
PLANT TO BASE
WITH TWINE

Pieces of bark, cork or simple wooden board can be adapted to provide an unusual container for an epiphyte. A common technique in the cultivation of *Platycerium* species, it can equally well be used to grow some of the larger, rhizome-rooted fern species. To provide a solid framework to support the rhizomes, an inch-thick layer of sphagnum moss is attached to the bark or board with plastic netting. The rhizomes of the fern are woven through the netting and secured to the moss. As with conventional hanging baskets, this type of planting will need frequent watering and regular misting. The moss should be kept moist at all times.

Using chicken wire, sphagnum moss and fern compost, a fern pole can be easily created to house a variety of epiphytes. A column of convenient height and width should be constructed from the chicken wire, and fastened securely where the ends meet. The inner surface is then covered with sphagnum moss, pushed against the wire to obliterate traces of the wire structure. Fill in the centre of the column with gritty fern compost, firmly compacted to remove air pockets. Select ferns with creeping rhizomes for planting, looping the rhizomes through the strands of wire. For display the pole can be suspended vertically from the ceiling or secured at floor level. This type of planting can be adapted to cover unsightly pillars in the greenhouse or conservatory, replacing bare wood or metal superstructures with a living, verdant cascade. Alternatively the pole can be attached horizontally across beams or superstructure.

As with basket cultivation, this type of planting will demand frequent watering and misting. However, observation of the condition of the moss will help to determine the need for moisture. While the moss is a deep green colour, watering will not be needed. A lightening of colour is a signal that watering will be required.

Ferns for baskets, rafts, plaques and fern poles

60°F (16°C) *Adiantum trapeziforme, Davallia fejeensis, Drymoglossum pilosel-loides, Drynaria quercifolia, Humata* spp., *Nephrolepis* spp., *Platycerium* spp., *Rumohra adiantiformis, Scyphularia pentaphylla.*

50°F (10°C) *Adiantum hispidulum, Adiantum raddianum, Aglaomorpha* spp., *Asplenium belangeri, Asplenium* spp., *Doodia aspera, Doodia maxima* (rasp fern), *Drynaria ridigula, Humata tyermannii* (hare's foot fern), *Lygodium palmatum, Nephrolepis acuminata* vars., *Nephrolepis cordifolia* vars. (fishbone fern), *N. exaltata* vars. (sword fern), *Pellaea* spp., *Pityrogramma argenta* (goldback fern), *Pityrogramma calomelanos* (silver fern), *P. chrysophylla, P. triangularis, Platycerium bifurcatum, P. veitchii, Pyrrosia* spp..

40°F (5°C) *Adiantum capillus-veneris* (common maidenhair fern), *Davallia canariensis* (hare's foot fern), *Lygodium japonicum, Pellaea atropurpurea, Polypodium australe, Pyrrosia lingua* (Japanese felt fern).

TERRARIUM CULTIVATION

The Ward case, or terrarium, was a delightful nineteenth-century innovation which, in recent years, has been rediscovered by many indoor gardeners. Initially it was used to conduct observations on chrysalis development, but Nathaniel Ward found that chance fern spores propagated and prospered within the confines of the sealed glass case. This discovery was the spur to the introduction of indoor fern cultivation in succeeding decades of the century. Prior to this, plant cultivation indoors had been confined to those few species which could withstand the conditions of the urban houses of that age, with their dark interiors and noxious fumes, emanating from gas lighting and coal fires.

Nineteenth-century examples of these cases were skilful pieces of craftsmanship and objects of some beauty in themselves. The more elaborate cases incorporated miniature fountains in their design. The Warrington case, an adaptation of the Ward case, proved extremely popular in Victorian times. This permitted accommodation for aquatic animals and ferns. Fortunately, such arcane structures, imprisoning small reptiles in artificial environments, have little appeal to modern tastes.

While the leaded-paned reproduction of Victorian Ward cases create fascinating objets d'art, it must be said that the smaller versions of these will not house a satisfying variety of ferns adequately. These small, widely available cases are best suited to containing one plant. To house a number of species, a larger construction is needed.

A practical, inexpensive fern case can be made from a redundant aquarium. A tank three feet in length by two feet wide and two feet deep will house up to 15 small species. The lid of the case should provide a close fit but should not seal the case hermetically. The base of the tank should be filled with at least three inches of coarse gravel to which a little granulated charcoal has been added. The soil should be made up of an equal mix of finely sifted, well-rotted leafmould, fibrous peat and fine grit or sharp sand. Sterilize the soil a day or so before use to avoid contamination of the case at a later stage by mould or fungi.

Small cases will need to be confined to either acid-preferring or alkaline-preferring species. Large terrariums will allow a variety of soil conditions to be incorporated within the case. Where alkaline-preferring species are to be grown, add a small quantity of ground lime or incorporate limestone chippings in the soil mix. A 4–6-inch layer of soil will be sufficient for most small ferns, leaving sufficient space between the top of the soil and the rim of the case.

Ideally, there should be a variety of contours within the terrarium if it is to be aesthetically pleasing. For alkaline-preferring species some sort of rockwork is by far the best solution, ensuring an attractive display and verisimilitude to natural growth. Small rocks, preferably all of the same type, should be collected and arranged within the tank before planting

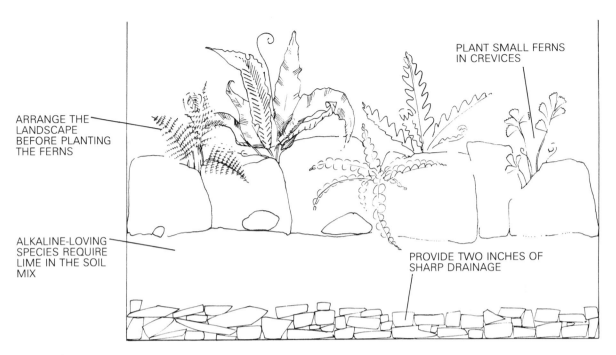

ARRANGE THE
LANDSCAPE
BEFORE PLANTING
THE FERNS

PLANT SMALL FERNS
IN CREVICES

ALKALINE-LOVING
SPECIES REQUIRE
LIME IN THE SOIL
MIX

PROVIDE TWO INCHES OF
SHARP DRAINAGE

Ward case

commences. It is well worth spending some time arranging the landscape of
the tank. Time and your own imagination are the only limitations when
creating a miniature fernery.

Many of the smaller rock-dwelling ferns are suitable for planting in these
sites. These ferns grow in fissures, supported by traces of soil blown into the
crevices. Their roots prefer to be lodged close to the rock, where they can
obtain a fairly constant seepage of moisture. Good planting will emulate the
natural habitat. Terrariums devoted to acid-preferring species can be landscaped with small branches, pieces of bark or logs. These should be free of
disease. Wrap sphagnum moss around them, securing the moss with nylon
fishing line or twine. Plant small epiphytes on the moss, adding a further
layer of moss, and secure with twine.

Planting is best undertaken in early spring, before the new fronds emerge.
If planting at other times, any damaged fronds should be cut off the plant.
Remove the fern from its pot and carefully wash traces of soil from the
roots. Firm the small roots into the crevices of the rockwork, securing them
with small splinters of rock and soil. Plants with ascending or erect crowns
should be planted so that their crowns are just above the surface of soil or
rock. Those with creeping rootstock will need their rhizomes lightly
covered with soil.

Water the case and replace the cover after planting is completed. Watering
should be done with care as there is no convenient way of removing excess
moisture. It may be better to under-water initially rather than risk saturating

the case. A hand-held sprayer, which will not disturb the soil, is the best method of watering. During the first few weeks monitor conditions within the case. If the moisture level is correct, condensation will form on the inside of the glass during the coolest parts of the day. Where the initial watering has been correct there will be no need to water again for some time. The need for further watering will be indicated by the absence of condensation on the glass. Maintenance is confined to the periodic removal of decayed fronds. There should be no need to feed the plants as the soil mix will supply sufficient nutrients. However, after a year or two, a light liquid feed could be given when replenishing the moisture content. Fern cases should be placed in light shade – diffused light from a northern window is ideal. Alternatively, artificial illumination can be provided by 'cool white' fluorescent tubes in locations where natural light levels are low.

Ferns for the terrarium

60°F   *Adiantum* spp., *Bolbotis heteroclita.*

50°F   *Actinopteris australis, Adiantum* spp., *Camptosorus rhizophyllus, Hymenophyllum* spp., *Trichomanes* spp., *Pteris* spp., *Woodsia* spp..

40°F   *Adiantum affine, Adiantum capillus-veneris, A. hispidulum, A. reniforme, Anogramma chaerophylla, Asplenium adiantum-nigrum, Asplenium ruta-muraria* (wall rue), *A. septentrionale, A. trichomanes (maidenhair spleenwort), A. viride, (green spleenwort), Athyrium distentifolium, Blechnum penna-marina, B. spicant, Cryptogramma crispa* (parsley fern)*, Cystopteris fragilis, C. montana, Gymnocarpium dryopteris, Gymnocarpium robertianum, Phyllitis scolopendrium* vars.*, Trichomanes Petersii, Trichomanes speciosum* (Killarney fern)*, Woodsia* spp..

HOUSE PLANTS

With care, some expertise and the correct provision of soil, temperature and humidity, almost all the small and medium sized species mentioned in this chapter can be grown in domestic settings. For the inexperienced gardener and for those who may not be able to devote quite as much time to cultivation needs as some of the more difficult subjects require, some reliance can be put on resilient species of fern for indoor display.

Most hardy ferns will tolerate the difficult conditions of domestic interiors. They should be placed out of doors for a week or so in bright shade at regular intervals during spring to autumn months to recuperate. Rotation of hardy plants between garden and room will sustain the vigour of the plants and maintain the freshness of the foliage. Tender ferns, in summer months, can also be rotated between garden and room. In the absence of a garden, a shady, north-facing balcony will suffice.

As in the greenhouse or conservatory, establishing plant groups will enhance the growing conditions of individual plants and reduce overall maintenance. However, single specimens of particularly fine or unusual forms can be particularly effective for decorating rooms. Here, double potting by enclosing pots in secondary, peat-filled containers can be effective in enhancing the overall humidity around the plant.

The hardy and relatively undemanding *Blechnum spicant* will make a striking and unusual house plant, with its compact rosette of barren fronds forming a counterpoint to the erect serrated fertile fronds. To create the maximum effect choose a shallow, 6-inch pan for the planting. A taller, equally easy plant is *Athyrium filix-femina* (lady fern). For indoor planting a choice should be made from the many fine crested and plumose varietal forms.

Although not as robust as some hardy ferns, *Asplenium bulbiferum* (mother and child fern) makes a particularly interesting house plant, its fronds producing a host of bulbils which may be harvested to produce a crop of further specimens. If an *Adiantum* species is desired, *A. hispidulum* (rosy maidenhair) will prove to be the best choice. It is the most undemanding of the *Adiantum* genera, with the bonus of pale red tints on the young fronds.

With its curious, furry rhizomes and fine triangular fronds *Davallia fejeensis* (rabbit's foot fern) is an ideal choice as a basket subject. *D. trichomanoides* has a more compact growth. Both are relatively easily grown.

Indoor ferns need not be confined to pans and baskets. Decorative logs and bark can be utilized as a planting medium for epiphytes. Hardy and semi-tender *Polypodium* will adapt more easily to room conditions than other epiphytes. Tie a sandwich of rough-textured fern compost and sphagnum moss to the log or bark. Peg down the creeping rhizomes to the moss, and cover for a week or so with polythene. When the fern has rooted itself to the moss, the polythene can be removed. In much the same fashion, moss-filled raffia baskets can be used to make unusual containers for these ferns. Maintenance will consist of keeping the moss moist at all times. As with most ferns in dwelling rooms, the plants should be sprayed regularly, and in summer placed outdoors in a shady spot.

9
PROPAGATION

Whether you intend to devote an extensive area to the cultivation of fern species, or merely desire to add ferns to existing planting schemes, you will at some stage wish to increase your stock of ferns. This need not be a daunting task, and can easily be undertaken by anyone who has mastered basic gardening skills.

Propagation from spores is the most effective method of raising large quantities of ferns from a parent plant. However, some cultivars, notably those of *Nephrolepis exaltata*, do not produce spores. Commercial horticulturalists propagate these types by tissue culture. On a smaller scale, vegetative propagation is the most practical method of increasing stocks of these plants, and is in fact the easiest method of raising small additional quantities of most ferns. This is achieved by division of crowns or layering of rhizomes. Alternatively, with some species the production of plantlets, stolons or bulbils can be exploited to provide a source of extra plants.

Whichever methods of propagation you adopt, some thought should be given to devoting a small area of the greenhouse or garden as a nursery bed. Here, young plants and recently propagated specimens can be closely monitored.

Tender ferns, even in warm climates, will need to be given the stable temperatures and humidity levels offered by the greenhouse or conservatory. Tender ferns in temperate areas will need, according to species, the shelter of the cool or warm greenhouse. A plunge bed in an area under staging, for example, where humidity is high and light levels are slightly lower than in the rest of the house, is an ideal site for a nursery bed. Depending on their size and rate of growth, tender ferns will need to spend one or two years in the greenhouse before being planted out in the garden. Harden off the plants in a sheltered, shaded coldframe or plunge bed for two weeks before planting out. This will allow plants to adapt to the lower humidity of the garden.

For hardy ferns, a coldframe built of brick or wood is the most practical form of nursery bed. The most convenient site outdoors will be adjacent to the garden shed or greenhouse, preferably offering the ferns a northern aspect. Where space and resources are limited, a simple plunge bed can be easily created in any shady corner of the garden.

Good drainage will be ensured by a three or four-inch layer of coarse grit or gravel. To this should be added an equal mix of peat and sharp sand to a depth sufficient to allow the potted ferns to be plunged up to their rims. Where the frame is to be covered by glass, allow some means of ensuring a good circulation of air around the plants. In all but the most deeply shaded site some form of plastic matting will be necessary to provide shade. A simple alternative to a glazed cover would be one constructed of wooden lathes. This has the merit of creating natural shading and allowing free circulation of air.

An alternative nursery bed for taller hardy ferns is a pit house. This is, simply, a rectangular pit dug in the ground. Dug to a depth of four feet and a span of three feet, with rudimentary steps to make access convenient, a pit house will provide good conditions for young and recuperating larger ferns. The work involved in the construction can be minimized if the pit is built into a north-facing slope. The floor of the pit should have a good depth of coarse drainage over which the plunge material is added. Such an enclosed area will offer stable levels of humidity and temperature. Wooden lathes or glazed frames covered with close-weave netting will give protection from excessive sun or heavy showers.

DIVISION OF ROOTSTOCK

Where only a few additional plants are required it will be generally more practical to divide established ferns. Specimens which have been grown for two or three years should be capable of being divided to produce three or four smaller plants. More mature plants will accommodate a greater degree of division. These more mature plants will benefit from division, since it is likely that the fronds are overcrowded and spoiling the symmetry of the plant.

Before division is undertaken, ascertain whether the fern to be divided has a vertical rootstock or a decumbent rhizome. The method of division in each type will be different.

The vertical or ascending type of rootstock is the most common type, seen in the *Adiantum*, *Athyrium*, *Dryopteris* and *Nephrolepis* species. From the rootstock, fronds arise in symmetrical or asymmetrical clusters. Symmetrical fronds arise from a central crown, as in *Athyrium* species. Asymmetrical fronds arise from a more or less densely packed clump, as in *Adiantum* species. As plants mature, further smaller crowns or clumps are produced around the initial frond base.

Decumbent rootstock develop creeping rhizomes which spread out underground to colonize further areas of the soil. These spreading or branching rhizomes throw up at intervals either individual fronds or clusters of fronds. Typical of this type of habit are the *Davallia*, *Gymnocarpium*, *Onoclea* and *Polypodium* species.

Division of clump-forming rootstock

The task of dividing the crowns of small plants is a relatively simple affair. Although division can be done at any time of year, early spring, before the fronds are unfurled, is generally the best time. At that time the rootstock and crowns are most visible, allowing clean divisions to be made. If division is made during the growing season some of the fronds of the divided ferns will need to be removed to reduce excessive loss of moisture.

Ferns are suitable for division when several smaller crowns or clumps have surrounded the main central crown or clump. Pot-grown ferns which are to be divided should be removed from their pots and the soil around the roots shaken off, taking care not to damage the fine roots. Determine the location of the ancillary growths and, using a sharp knife, prise apart each of the small clumps, together with a section of root. Do not cut into the individual clumps. Where several ferns are being divided, cover the divided plants with damp moss or wet newspaper to keep them moist until they are repotted.

The donor fern should be repotted in the original pot using fresh fern compost. The immature crowns obtained from the division should be potted in small pots, with their crowns just above the level of the soil. Two or three-inch pots incorporating an inch of drainage material should be sufficient for small specimens. A potting mix of one part finely sieved leafmould and one part sand will ensure a balance of good drainage and moisture retentiveness. Water the ferns thoroughly and plunge them in a nursery bed for their first year. The newly potted ferns should be kept moist, but not wet. Ensure that you maintain a good balance of ventilation and humidity around the plants.

Plants grown in open ground will need to be removed from the soil prior to division. Carefully excavate the soil around the fern to determine the extent of its roots. This is likely to be at least half the spread of the fronds. Lift the plant together with the soil ball, and carefully remove the soil from around the roots. If necessary wash away surplus soil to reveal the crowns and the roots. The technique applied to the division of pot-grown ferns should be followed. More robust specimens may need to be divided by inserting two garden forks back-to-back between crowns to force them apart. Further divisions may be made using the same technique until the required number of divisions are made. Most established plants should generate three or four small plants. Vigorous specimens may yield more.

The parent plant can be replaced in the permanent planting site if moist, shady growing conditions are present. However, the small divided ferns benefit from being placed in a shaded, sheltered area to develop for a further year. In either case the site should be prepared by the addition of a good quantity of rotted leafmould and grit. The additional leafmould will ensure that the young ferns will have sufficient moisture on hand to sustain them while their root structure develops. The ferns should be planted so that their crowns are just above the level of the soil. Water the ground generously around the plants and ensure that the soil does not dry out during the following months.

Division of decumbent rootstock

The division of ferns with creeping rhizomes is achieved by severing lengths of the rootstock which have one or two growing tips. The soil around the plant which is to be divided should be carefully excavated to reveal the rhizome. Providing the parent plant has developed sufficiently to withstand division, two-inch sections which reveal growing buds can be removed with a sharp knife. Ideally, separated sections should have at least some trace of root along their length. Sections without roots but with budding points will take longer to establish themselves and will need to be pegged down to the soil. The separated sections should be cleaned and treated with a mild fungicide at the cut ends. Plant to the same depth as the parent plant in shallow pans or boxes containing good drainage and a mix of one part fine grit and one part well-rotted leafmould. Water thoroughly and cover the container with glass or some translucent material to ensure humidity. Tender species should be placed in a shaded area of the greenhouse. Hardy species can be housed in a frame or plunge bed. In both situations, remove the cover of the container for a short period to increase ventilation if any sign of mould is evident on the soil. Water the plants if the soil shows signs of becoming dry, but avoid keeping the soil constantly soggy.

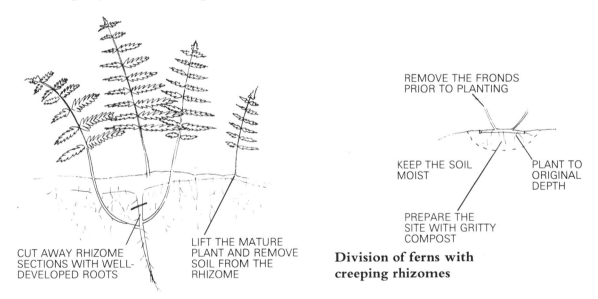

CUT AWAY RHIZOME SECTIONS WITH WELL-DEVELOPED ROOTS

LIFT THE MATURE PLANT AND REMOVE SOIL FROM THE RHIZOME

REMOVE THE FRONDS PRIOR TO PLANTING

KEEP THE SOIL MOIST

PLANT TO ORIGINAL DEPTH

PREPARE THE SITE WITH GRITTY COMPOST

Division of ferns with creeping rhizomes

PLANTLETS AND BULBILS

Some ferns, notably *Asplenium bulbiferum* (mother and child fern), *Camptosorus rhizophyllus* (walking fern), *Platycerium* (stag's horn fern), *Polystichum setiferum*, and some species of *Woodwardia* produce plantlets or bulbils – tiny clusters of tissue – at the base of the frond or along the midrib or at the apex. These embryonic plants offer a further source of increasing stock.

Plantlets and bulbils can be carefully removed from the parent plant with a sharp knife. Press the plantlets or bulbils onto the soil so that they are partly submerged in the planting mix. Shallow pans with an inch of good drainage and a compost containing an equal mix of finely sieved leafmould and sharp sand or grit are most suitable. Water the pan thoroughly and place it in a shaded site. Ensure sufficient humidity by covering the pan with glass. If heavy condensation forms on the glass, remove the cover to allow excess moisture to evaporate. From these bulbils small ferns will develop. When the ferns are large enough to handle, remove them from the pan and pot up into separate pots. Keep the newly potted plants in the nursery bed for a year before establishing them elsewhere.

An alternative method is to peg down a frond bearing either a plantlet or bulbils, and cover it lightly with soil. For pot-grown specimens, the bulbil should be pegged down in a small pot containing an equal mixture of sharp sand and well-rotted leafmould. This method allows the bulbil to continue to receive moisture from the parent plant while it develops an independent root system. When the root system is sufficiently developed, sever the new plant from the parent frond. This procedure should be used to propagate from the thin, green stolons produced by *Nephrolepis* species.

Propagation of offsets from
Camptosorus rhizophyllus

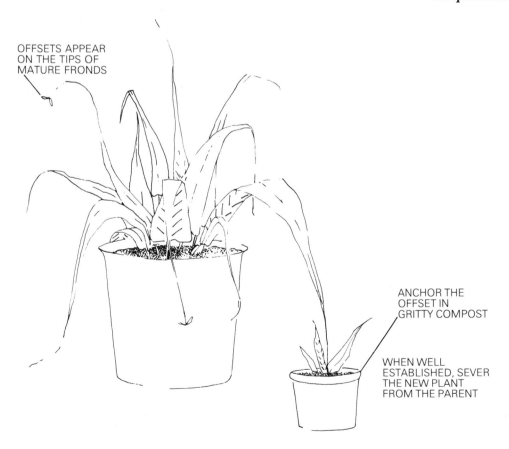

OFFSETS APPEAR
ON THE TIPS OF
MATURE FRONDS

ANCHOR THE
OFFSET IN
GRITTY COMPOST

WHEN WELL
ESTABLISHED, SEVER
THE NEW PLANT
FROM THE PARENT

PROPAGATION BY SPORES

Where large numbers of plants are required, spore propogation will prove to be the most efficient means. Although this is the most challenging aspect of fern cultivation, it is also the most rewarding. Offsetting the time and patience which are involved in raising plants from spores is the ever-present prospect that there may emerge from any batch of young plants a new variety which may exhibit a particularly fine form.

Not only will spore propagation increase existing fern stocks, but raising ferns from spores also allows the enthusiast the opportunity to acquire other fern species by participating in world-wide spore distribution networks. In this way ferns which are difficult to obtain locally can be raised in quantity.

The key to successful propagation from spores lies in observing scrupulous cleanliness at each stage. The unwanted airborne spores of fungi and mosses will quickly overwhelm the sporeling at an early stage if containers and compost are not kept sterile.

Collecting spores

In late summer the fertile fronds of ferns will show the characteristic spore clusters on the underside of the fronds or, with some species, in clusters along the rachis of fertile fronds. Initially green at first, the spore clusters darken to a rust colour before becoming dark brown. Spores should be collected just before the sporangia burst open to release the mature spores. Examination with a hand lens will help to determine the optimum time for collection – when the spore cases, the sporangia, are dark brown but not yet broken.

The simplest method of collecting spores is to detach part of a fertile frond and carefully insert it into a small envelope or plastic bag. This should be kept in a dry room for a few days for the spores to be released from the sporangia. At the end of that time a quantity of dust-like particles will be seen at the bottom of the container. These are the spores.

The spores can be sown immediately or kept for sowing at a more convenient time. Apart from the spores of the *Osmunda*, *Todea* and *Leptopteris* species, which are viable for only a few days, spores can be kept for several years before being propagated. However the greatest success will come from spores sown soon after collection.

Sowing spores

There are several methods of sowing spores. However, all depend for their success on ensuring that containers and compost are sterilized, and remain free from airborne contamination by other organisms which will inhibit the development of the spores.

The materials you will need are sterilized containers, the standard fern compost mixture or commercial compost, and some panes of glass or polythene to cover the containers.

Containers with good drainage should be selected and thoroughly cleaned to remove any trace of previous plant material and compost. The container should then be sterilized by plunging it in boiling water for several minutes. Any container which will not distort with this treatment will be satisfactory. Shallow clay pans are generally the most suitable.

If the compost for propagation is the standard fern mixture this should be sifted into a coarse and a fine grade. Layer the bottom of the container with the coarse grade of compost. The fine grade compost is used to top up the container to within a half inch of the rim. Cover the container with kitchen tissue and pour boiling water onto it. The tissue will prevent the soil from washing out of the pan. Remove the tissue, replacing it with a previously sterilized glass or polythene cover to ensure the container does not become contaminated by airborne organisms.

When the soil has cooled and the spores are to hand, remove the glass or cling-film. Distribute the spores evenly over the surface of the soil. Do not spread them too thickly or you may have trouble separating the plantlets at the pricking-out stage. The covering should be speedily replaced after the spores have been sown. The container should be kept in a sheltered spot and covered to exclude the light – newspaper or a piece of sacking will do. The optimum temperature for spore propagation is 65–70°F (18–21°C). If propagated in spring, the spores of hardy species can succeed in containers placed outdoors in sheltered, shaded cold frames.

At no time must the soil be allowed to dry out. Check the containers periodically to ensure that the compost remains moist. If additional moisture is required, replenish with water which has been previously boiled, and apply with a hand sprayer.

After a period of time, generally one to two weeks but varying according to the fern species, the compost will have the appearance of being covered with a green mould. At this stage the lightproof cover can be removed. The presence of this growth indicates that the spores have germinated. During this stage the prothallus develops female organs (Archegonia), containing the eggs, and male organs (Antheridia), containing the sperm. Moisture on the surface of the soil will allow the sperm to swim to the eggs and fertilize them. The container should not be exposed to the air and the glass or polythene cover must remain to protect the plants at this critical time.

After some months a first leaf will develop out of the prothallus. At this stage the glass or polythene covering can be removed, though the plants should remain sheltered from direct sunlight. After a further period secondary leaves, resembling those of the parent plant, will appear and the new plant will start to develop a root system independent of the prothallus. At this stage the prothallus itself will begin to wither and disappear. If the young ferns are not too closely spaced they can be left for a further few months to develop their root systems. More densely packed plants should be carefully pricked out and replanted in a similar potting mixture. Ten or so young ferns can be accommodated round the circumference of a shallow six-inch pan. These can be grown on in a nursery bed for a further one or two years.

An alternative method of spore propagation which dispenses with compost can be tried. The medium which is substituted for the compost can be a house brick, an inverted clay pot or a small paving stone. Whichever medium is chosen, it should be placed on a shallow dish and sterilized with boiling water. Sterilize the surface on which the dish is to stand as well. Cover with a bell jar or clear kitchen mixing bowl and allow to cool. When all is cool uncover the bowl and sow the spores thinly on the pot or brick. Replace the bowl as quickly as possible.

The water in the dish will keep the clay sufficiently moist for the spores to develop and the prothalli to grow. If a clay pot is used fill the interior with sphagnum moss before inverting it on the dish. This will ensure an evenly moist surface. If necessary, replenish the water reservoir in the dish with water which has previously been boiled.

After fertilization, when the ferns are seen to have developed their first small frond, each fern, with its shrivelling prothalli, can be carefully removed with a sharp knife. Plant the young ferns into shallow pans. Several plants can be accommodated in six-inch pans. This method is useful where small numbers of ferns are required. Where large numbers are wanted, the task of removing the ferns from the sides of pots or bricks may prove to be too time consuming to justify the use of this method.

Problems in spore propagation

The most frequent source of problems experienced in spore propagation is contamination by other organisms. This reveals itself in the invasion of the compost by mosses and fungi. These will overwhelm the embryonic prothalli and arrest any further development. In these circumstances there is little hope of achieving success with that particular sowing. Rather, it will be best to review sterilization procedures and attempt a second sowing.

Contamination can occur at any stage. It may be due to insufficient sterilization of the container or the compost. Frequently, contamination occurs when the cover of the container is removed for watering. It may be more prudent to replenish the moisture by placing the covered container on a dish of water for half an hour. However, do not keep the container permanently resting in water.

The successful formation of mature prothalli, evident as green wedge-shaped growths $\frac{1}{4}$in. (0.6cm) in size, should be followed some weeks after by the emergence on the prothalli of small fronds. An initial single leaf is followed by the growth of more recognizable tiny fronds. If there is insufficient moisture on the surface of the prothallus, fertilization cannot take place. The male sperms, contained in the antheridia, require a film of moisture to swim across the prothallus to the archegonia, in order to fertilize the female eggs.

In this situation, fertilization of mature prothalli can be induced by applying a fine spray of water at 65°F (18°C) over the surface of the prothalli. Repeat at weekly intervals until there are signs of successful fertilization. A fine spray of water is all that is required. Avoid waterlogging the soil.

10
LIST OF CULTIVATED FERNS

Acrostichum, 3 species, large fern, pantropical.
Habitat – salt water and mangrove swamps; erect
rhizome. **Cultivation** – open shade, boggy, acid soil,
can be treated as an aquatic. **Propagate** by spores.

A. aureum, leather fern, tropics, 3–8ft (0.9–2.4m), 60°F
(16°C).
A. danaeifolium syn. *A. excelcum*, swamp fern, tropics,
5–13ft (1.5–4m), 60°F (16°C).

Actinopteris, 3 species, small fern, tropical Africa.
Habitat – open semi-arid area; creeping rhizome.
Cultivation – likes warm, dry conditions and a very
free-draining compost. **Propagate** by spores and
division. Related to *Cheilanthes*.

A. australis syn. *A. radiata*, S&E Africa, Arabia and
India, 4–10in. (10–25cm), 60°F (16°C).
A. semiflabellata, S&E Africa, Arabia and India, 12in.
(30cm), 60°F (16°C).

Adiantum, from the Greek 'a', not, and 'diantos',
moistened, the fronds were reputed to remain dry
when plunged into water; 200 species, small/medium
fern, worldwide distribution. **Habitat** – cliffs,
crevices, waterfalls and shady stream banks; creeping
or ascending rhizome. **Cultivation** – indoor
terrarium, baskets and pots. Requires a moist,
well-drained soil; avoid wetting fronds. **Propagate**
by spores and division.

A. aethiopicum, Australia, tropical Africa and America,
16in. (41cm), 50°F (10°C).
A. affine, N.Z., 6–9in. (16–23cm), 50°F (10°C).
A. asarifolium, Mascarene islands, 20in. (51cm), 50°F
(10°C).
A. capillus-veneris, common maidenhair, N. America
and Europe, 6in. (16cm), 40°F (5°C), alkaline soil.
A. caudatum, tropical Asia and Japan, 12–18in.
(30–46cm), 60°F (16°C).
A. concinnum, C&N South America, 24in. (60cm),
60°F (16°C)
A. cristatum, West Indies, 6–12in. (16–30cm), 60°F
(16°C).

A. cultratum, tropical America, 12in. (30cm), 60°F
(16°C).
A. cuneatum syn. *A. raddianum*, American and African
tropics, 8–12in. (20–30cm), 50°F (10°C).
A. cunninghamii, tropical & subtropical Australia, 10in.
(25cm), 50°F (10°C).
A. diaphanum, Indonesia, Australasia and Pacific
Islands, 4–8in. (10–20cm), 50°F (10°C).
A. excisum, Chile, Bolivia, 10in. (25cm), 60°F
(16°C).
A. formosum, tropical & subtropical Australia, N.Z.,
30in. (76cm), 50°F (10°C).
A. fulvum, Polynesia, 6–9in. (16–23cm), 50°F (10°C).
A. gracillimum, S. Europe, 9–24in. (23–61cm), 50°F
(10°C).
A. hispidulum, rosy maidenhair, E. Africa, SE Asia,
N.Z., 8–16in. (20–41cm), 40°F (6°C), young fronds
rose coloured.
A. incisum, C. Africa, 12in. (30cm), 50°F (10°C).
A. jordanii, California maidenhair, Western N.
America, from Oregon to Mexico, 12in. (30cm),
50°F (10°C).
A. latifolium, tropical America, West Indies, 6–12in.
(16–30cm), 60°F (16°C).
A. macrophyllum, C&S America, 6–12in. (16–30cm),
60°F (16°C).
A. monochlamys, Japan, 6–9in. (16–23cm), 40°F (5°C).
A. Moorei, Peru, 6–15in. (16–38cm), 60°F (16°C).
A. palmatum, Peru, 36in. (90cm), 50°F (10°C).
A. patens, tropical America, 6–9in. (16–23cm), 60°F
(16°C).
A. pedatum, N. America, NE Asia, 9–18in. (23–46cm),
hardy, several cultivars.
A. peruvianum, tropical S. America, Ecuador, Bolivia,
3–4in (7–10cm), 60°F (16°C).
A. polyphyllum, subtropical America, Colombia and
Venezuela, 18–36in. (46–90cm), 60°F (16°C).
A. pulverulentum, tropical America and West Indies,
6–12in. (16–30cm), 60°F (16°C).
A. raddianum syn. *A. cuneatum*, delta maidenhair,
American and African tropics, 8–12in. (20–30cm),

50°F (10°C), evergreen, several cultivars.

A. reniforme, Canary islands, 2in. (5cm), 50°F (10°C).

A. sylvaticum, E. Australia, 18in. (46cm), 50°F (10°C).

A. tenerum brittle maidenhair, N. America, C&S America, W. Indies, 18–36in. (46–90cm), 40°F (5°C), many cultivars.

A. trapeziforme, syn. *A. pentadactylon*, tropical America, 18–36in. (46–90cm), 60°F (16°C), many cultivars.

A. venustum, Himalaya, 12in. (30cm), hardy.

Aglaomorpha, 10 species, large fern, Formosa, Malaysia. **Habitat** – epiphytic on rocks; creeping rhizome. **Cultivation** – baskets and rafts in gritty soil, suited to warm, humid, large area. **Propagate** by spores and division.

A. coronans syn. *Polypodium coronans*, S. Himalaya to N. Malaysia, 6ft (1.8m), 50°F (10°C).

A. heraclea syn. *Polypodium heracleum*, Malaysia, 6ft (1.8m), 50°F (10°C).

A. meyeniana, bear's paw, Philippines to Taiwan, 2–3ft (61–91cm), 50°F (10°C).

Alsophila, from Gr. 'alsos', a grove, and 'philos', to love, an allusion to its typical habitat; 30 species, tropics, large fern. **Habitat** – cloud forests, mountain slopes, ravines and streamsides; erect rhizome. **Cultivation** – large pots or open beds in moist, free-draining soil. **Propagate** by spores.

A. australis syn. *Cyathea australis*, Australian tree fern, Australia, fronds to 14ft (4m) trunk to 40ft (12m), 60°F (16°C).

A. tricolor syn *Cyathea dealbata*, N.Z., trunk 30ft (9m), fronds 3–9ft (0.9–2.7m), 50°F (10°C).

Ampelopteris, from Gr. 'ampelos', a vine, and 'opsis', resemblance, a reference to its scandent habit; 1 species, W. Africa to NE Australia, large fern. **Habitat** – riverbanks and ditches; creeping rhizome. **Cultivation** – sunny sites in moist soil. Spreads extensively. **Propagate** by division.

A. prolifera, tropical Asia 36–48in. (90–120cm), 50°F (10°C).

Anemia, from Gr. 'aneimon', naked, a reference to the uncovered sori; 90 species, tropics and subtropics, small/medium fern. **Habitat** – open well-drained sites, ravines, rocky outcrops; creeping rhizome. **Cultivation** – bright, open shade in well-drained soil. **Propagate** by spores.

A. adiantifolia, pine fern, Florida, West Indies, western S. America, 10–20in. (25–51cm), 40°F (50°C).

A. mexicana, Texas, 12–24in. (30–60cm), 60°F (16°C).

A. phyllitidis, flowering fern, West Indies, C. America to Cuba, 12–24in. (30–60cm), 40°F (5°C).

A. rotundifolia, Brazil, 12in. (30cm), 50°F (10°C).

Angiopteris, 1 species, tropical Asia and Polynesia, large fern. **Habitat** – wet forests; erect rhizome. **Cultivation** – moist soil. **Propagate** by spores and stipules. Related to *Marattia*.

A. evecta, Madagascar to Polynesia, Japan and Australia, fronds 5ft (1.5cm), stems 2–8ft (0.6–2.4m), 60°F (16°C), evergreen.

Anogramma, 7 species, tropical and temperate, small fern. **Habitat** – wet ravines, edges of pools, on moist rocky banks. **Cultivation** – as terrarium plants. Heavy shade and a moist soil. A rapid growing, annual fern. **Propagate** by spores.

A. chaerophylla, Mexico, 12in. (30cm), 50°F (10°C).

A. leptophylla, temperate regions, 2–3in. (5–7cm), hardy.

Anopteris, 1 species, large fern, Bermuda, Cuba, Jamaica. **Habitat** – limestone cliffs and ravines in wet forests; ascending rhizome. **Cultivation** – warm, humid, permanently moist sites. Requires large space. **Propagate** by spores and bulbils.

A. evecta syn. *A. hexagona*, tropical America and Asia, caudex 2ft (0.6m), fronds 6–10ft (1.8–3m), 60°F (16°C).

Arachnioides, 50 species, tropics and subtropics, medium fern. **Habitat** – ravines in wet forests; creeping rhizome. Cultivation – pots and beds in a moist soil. **Propagate** by spores and division.

A. aristata, East Indian holly fern, Japan to Australia and Polynesia, 12–36in. (30–90cm), 50°F (10°C).

Aspidotis, 4 species, small fern, America and Africa. **Habitat** – rocks and cliffs; ascending rhizome. **Cultivation** as for *Cheilanthes*. **Propagate** by spores and division. Considered by some authorities now to belong to the *Cheilanthes* genera. Includes:

A. californica, C. America, 12in. (30cm), 50°F (10°C).

A. densa, pod fern, tropical America, 10in. (25cm), 50°F (10°C).

Asplenium, from Gr. 'a', not, and 'splene', spleen, an allusion to *A. adiantum-nigrum*, reputed to cure diseases of the spleen; 650 species, small/medium fern, worldwide, terrestial and epiphytic. **Habitat** – ravines, rocks and cliffs in moist forests; ascending rhizome. **Cultivation** – walls, rockeries, terrarium and pots. Light shade, moist, free-draining (mostly alkaline) soil. **Propagate** by spores and division.

A. adiantum-nigrum, black spleenwort, temperate Europe, 3–18in. (7–96cm), calcareous soil, hardy.

*A.*x. *alternifolium*, alternate-leaved spleenwort, temperate Europe, 6in. (16cm), calcareous soil, hardy.

A. attenuatum, E. Australia, 3–4in. (7–10cm), 50°F (10°C), viviparous.

A. auritum, tropical America, 12in. (30cm), 60°F (16°C).

A. belangeri, Malaysia, Indonesia, China, 4–30in. (10–76cm), 60°F (16°C).

A. billotii, lanceolate spleenwort, Europe, 6in. (16cm), hardy.

A. bulbiferum, mother fern, Malaya, Australia, N.Z., 12–24in. (30–60cm), 40°F (5°C), acid soil.

A. daucifolium, viviparous, Madagascar, Mauritius, Reunion, 10–15in. (25–38cm), 50°F (10°C), acid soil.

A. falcatum, S.E. Asia, Australasia, 36in. (90cm), 40°F (5°C).

A. flabellifolium, Australia, N.Z., 6–12in. (16–30cm), 40°F (5°C), baskets.

A. flaccidum, hanging spleenwort, Australia, N.Z., 12–36in. (30–90cm), 40°F (5°C), baskets.

A. fontanum, S&C Europe, 3–6in. (7–16cm), 40°F (5°C).

A. formosum, tropics, 12–18in. (30–46cm), 60°F (16°C).

A. friesiorum, tropical Africa, 12in. (30cm), 60°F (16°C).

A. longissimum, Indonesia, 2–8ft (0.6–2.4m), 60°F 16(°C).

A. lucidum, N.Z., 24in. (60cm), 50°F (10°C).

A. marinum, sea spleenwort, coasts of Europe, Atlantic Islands, 4in. (10cm), 40°F (5°C).

A. montanum, N. America, 2–6in. (5–16cm), 40°F (5°C).

A. nidus, bird's nest, old world tropics, 12–48in. (30–120cm), 50°F (10°C), acid soil.

A. palmatum syn. *A. hemionitis*, Atlantic Islands, N. Africa and Portugal, 4–8in. (10–20cm), 40°F (5°C).

A. platyneuron, ebony spleenwort, N. America, 8–15in. (20–38cm), calcareous soil, 40°F (5°C), will withstand full sun.

A. ruta-muraria, wall rue, temperate Europe, N. America, 2–4in. (5–10cm), calcareous soil, hardy.

A. septentrionale, forked spleenwort, temperate Europe, 2–5in. (5–15cm), calcareous soil, hardy.

A. squamulatum, Malaysia, 18in. (46cm), 60°F (16°C).

A. stuhlmannii, E. Africa, 8–18in. (20–46cm), 60°F (16°C).

A. trichomanes subsp. *quadrivalens*, common maidenhair spleenwort, n&s temperate regions, calcareous soil, 6in. (16cm), hardy, will withstand full sun.

A. trichomanes subsp. *trichomanes*, delicate maidenhair spleenwort, n&s temperate regions, 6in. (16cm), calcareous soil, hardy.

A. viride, green spleenwort, northern temperate regions, calcareous soil, 2–6in. (5–16cm), hardy.

A. viviparum, Mascarene Islands, 6–9in. (16–23cm), 60°F (16°C), calcareous soil, viviparous.

Athyrium, 500 species, medium/large fern, worldwide. **Habitat** – woodland; ascending rhizome. **Cultivation** – in beds and pots in moist, acid soil. **Propagate** by spores and division.

A. australe, Australia, N.Z., 8–16in. (20–41cm), 40°F (5°C).

A. distentifolium syn. *A. alpestre*, N. America, temperate Europe, 12–30in. (30–76cm), hardy.

A. filix-femina, woodland lady fern, N. Europe, N. America, 15–36in. (38–90cm), hardy, many cultivars.

A. flexile, flexile lady fern, N. Europe, 9in. (23cm), hardy.

A. nipponicum 'pictum' syn. *A. goeringianum* 'pictum', Japanese painted fern, 24in. (60cm), hardy.

A. japonicum. Australasia, N.Z., 12–24in. (30–60cm), 40°F (5°C).

A. nipponicum syn. *A. goeringianum*, China, Japan, Taiwan, 9–36in. (23–90cm), hardy.

A. pycnocarpon syn. *Diplazium pycnocarpon*, glade fern, N. America, 24–36in. (60–90cm), hardy.

A. thelypteroides, silver glade fern, N. America, 36in. (90cm), hardy.

Azolla, from Gr. 'azo', to dry, and 'ollo', to kill, an allusion to its need for an aquatic habitat; 6 species, small fern, world-wide. **Habitat** – aquatic; creeping rhizome. **Cultivation** – pools and pans containing wet, acid soil. **Propagate** by division. Dies back in winter.

A. caroliniana, temperate America, $\frac{1}{4}$in. (64mm), 40°F (5°C).

A. filiculoides, tropical America, $\frac{1}{4}$–2in. (.6–5cm), 40°F (5°C).

A. mexicana, western N. America to Bolivia, 4–6in. (10–16cm), 40°F (5°C).

Belvisia, 25 species, small fern, Africa to Polynesia. **Habitat** – epiphytic on rocks; creeping rhizome. **Cultivation** – epiphytic sites in warm, humid areas. **Propagate** by spores and division. Treat as *Polypodium*.

B. mucronata, Sri Lanka to Australia, Polynesia, 4in. (10cm), 60°F (16°C).

Blechnum, from Gr. 'blechnon', a fern; 200 species, medium/large fern, S. hemisphere tropics and temperate regions. **Habitat** – wet mountain forest, swamps, thickets. In tropics grows in lowland rain forests, cloud forests and ravines, streambanks and rivers; creeping, erect or trunk-forming rhizome. **Cultivation** – as ground cover or as 'accent' plants in containers. Good light, but not strong sun. Moist, wet soil. Susceptible to fungus leaf spot, mealy bugs and scale insect. **Propagate** by spores and division.

B. auriculatum, temperate S. America, 24in. (60cm), 50°F (10°C).

B. brasiliense, tropical S. America, fronds 3–4ft (0.9–1.2m), trunk to 3ft (90cm), 50°F (10°C).

B. capense, South Africa, 3ft (90cm), 60°F (16°C).

B. cartilagineum, E. Australia, 5ft (1.5m), 40°F (5°C).

B. discolor, Australia, 3ft (90cm), 50°F (10°C).

B. fluviatile, SE Australia, N.Z., 20in. (51cm), 40°F (5°C).

B. gibbum, New Caledonia and New Hebrides, fronds 3–4ft (0.9–1.2m), trunk to 3ft (90cm), 50°F (10°C).

B. moorei, New Caledonia, fronds 3ft (90cm), 50°F (10°C).

B. nipponicum, N. Japan, 12in. (30cm), hardy.

B. nudum, E. Australia, N.Z., fronds 15–24in. (38–60cm), trunk to 3ft (90cm), 40°F (5°C).

B. occidentale, hammock fern, tropical America, Pacific islands, fronds 12–16in. (30–41cm), 50°F (10°C).

B. orientale, tropical Asia, Australasia, Pacific, fronds 4½ft (1.4m), trunk 24in. (61cm), 60°F (16°C).

B. patersonii, N.Z., 16in. (41cm), 40°F (5°C).

B. penna-marina, N.Z., 4–8in. (10–20cm), 40°F (5°C).

B. serrulatum, saw fern, Florida, Australasia, fronds 24in. (60cm), trunk 12in. (30cm), 60°F (16°C).

B. spicant, hard fern/deer fern, N. America, Europe, N. Asia, 24in. (60cm), hardy.

B. tabulare, southern S. America, Falkland Islands, 3–4ft (0.9–1.2m), hardy.

Bolbotis, 85 species, small/medium fern, tropical America. **Habitat** – wet to seasonally dry, shaded forests and along water courses; creeping rhizome. **Cultivation** – as aquatic or epiphyte. **Propagate** by spores and division.

B. heteroclita, tropical SE Asia, 8–12in. (20–30cm), 60°F (16°C).

Botrychium, 40 species, worldwide, small/medium fern. **Habitat** – open grassland, meadows in neutral to sub-acidic soil; ascending rhizome. **Cultivation** – beds and borders in well-drained acid soil. **Propagate** by spores and division.

B. dissectum, cut-leaved grape fern, 6–15in. (16–38cm), hardy.

B. lunaria, moonwort, N. America, 3–9in. (7–23cm), hardy.

B. matricariifolium syn. *B. ramosum*, daisy-leaf grape fern, 6in. (16cm), hardy.

B. multifidum, leather fern, N. America, 12–18in. (30–45cm), hardy.

B. virginianum, rattlesnake fern, N. America, 5–12in. (15–30cm), hardy.

Camptosorus, 2 species, medium fern, ascending rhizome, N. America, NE Asia. **Habitat** – wet rocks. **Cultivation** – rock gardens and terrarium with moist, alkaline soil. A short-lived fern susceptible to slug damage. **Propagate** by spores and offsets.

C. rhizophyllus, walking fern, N. America, 6–12in. (16–30cm), 40°F (5°C).

Campyloneurum, 20 species, large fern, tropical America. **Habitat** – epiphytic in humid forests, among rocks in upland areas; creeping rhizome. **Cultivation** – as epiphyte in baskets with gritty soil. **Propagate** by spores and division.

C. phyllitidis, syn. of *Pleopeltis phyllitidis*, strap fern, tropical America, 18in. (46cm), 60°F (16°C).

Ceratopteris, from Gr. 'keras', a horn, and 'pteris', a fern, a reference to the shape of the sterile fronds; 3 species, small fern, pantropical. **Habitat** – aquatic in ditches, lagoons and marshes; creeping rhizome. **Cultivation** as aquatic in pools. **Propagate** by division.

C. pteridoides, water fern, sub-tropical and tropical America, 6–12in. (16–30cm), 60°F (16°C).

C. thalictroides, American tropics, 6–12in. (16–30cm), 60°F (16°C), viviparous.

Ceterach, 10 species, small fern, Europe and temperate Asia. **Habitat** – rocks and walls. **Cultivation** – light, open shade in well-drained, rocky soil. **Propagate** by spores and division.

C. aureum, rusty-back fern, Madeira, Canary islands, 9in. (23cm), 40°F (5°C).

C. dalhousiae, Himalayas, acid soil, 7–10in. (18–25cm), 40°F (5°C).

C. officinarum, rusty-back fern (scale fern), Eurasia, alkaline soil, 6in. (16cm), hardy.

Cheilanthes, from Gr. 'cheilos', a lip, and 'anthos', a flower, referring to the indusium; 180 species, small, evergreen fern, temperate regions and tropics.

Habitat – open, semi-arid areas, cliffs, ledges, and stone walls; creeping rhizome. **Cultivation** – dry, sunny, undisturbed site in slightly acid soil. Resents overwatering. Shortlived. **Propagate** by spores and division.

C. Alabamensis, N. America, alkaline soil, 4–12in. (10–30cm), 40°F (5°C).

C. argentea, E. Asia, 6–10in. (16–25cm), 40°F (6°C).

C. farinosa, E. Africa, SW Asia, 3–12in. (7–30cm), 50°F (10°C).

C. Feei, N. America, alkaline soil, 4–12in. (10–30cm), 40°F (5°C).

C. fragrans syn. *C. pteridioides*, lip fern, Mediterranean, 2–5in. (5–15cm), 40°F (6°C).

C. gracillima, lace fern, N. America, 4–8in. (10–20cm), 40°F (5°C).

C. lanosa, hairy lip fern, N. America, 6–8in. (16–20cm), 40°F (5°C).

C. pulchella, Canary islands, 4–6in. (10–16cm), 40°F (6°C).

C. tomentosa, S. America, acidic soil, 6–16in. (16–41cm), 40°F (5°C).

Cibotium, 8 species, large fern, Asia, Hawaiian islands and C. America. **Habitat** – thickets and forests of tropical mountains, wooded slopes and ravines; erect trunk-forming rhizome. **Cultivation** – 'accent' plant in beds and pots in moist, acid soil. **Propagate** by spores.

C. Barometz, Scythian lamb fern, China, Taiwan, SE Asia, 4–5ft (1.2–1.5m), 60°F (16°C).

C. chamissoi, Hawaii, fronds to 6ft (1.8m), 60°F (16°C).

C. glaucum, Hawaiian tree fern, Hawaii, 15ft (4.5m), fronds 6ft (1.8m) wide, 60°F (16°C).

C. schiedei, Mexican tree fern, C. America, 3–4ft (0.9–1.2m) fronds to 6ft (1.8m), 60°F (16°C).

Cryptogramma, from Gr. 'kryptos', hidden, and 'gramme', a line, a reference to indusium; 5 species, small fern, Europe, Asia and N. America. **Habitat** – lime-free scree; creeping rhizome. **Cultivation** – light, humid, open conditions in well-drained, lime-free rock garden or terrarium. **Propagate** by spores and division.

C. acrostichoides, N. America, 2in. (5cm), hardy.

C. crispa, parsley fern, Europe & SW Asia, 6–8in. (16–20cm), hardy.

C. Stelleri, slender cliff brake, N. America, calcareous rocks, 1–2in. (2–5cm), hardy.

Ctenitis, 130 species, pantropics. **Habitat** – cloud forests, ravines, water courses and mountain slopes; medium/large fern, creeping/erect rhizome. **Cultivation** – moist free-draining soil. **Propagate** by spores.

C. decomposita syn. *C. pentangularis*, N.Z. and Australia, fronds 36in. (91cm), 50°F (10°C).

C. Sloanei, comb fern, Florida, stem 18in. (46cm), fronds to 12ft (3.7m), 60°F (16°C).

Culcita, 10 species, temperate and tropical regions. **Habitat** – forests, thickets and clearings; medium/large fern, creeping rhizome. **Cultivation** – open sites in well-drained soil. **Propagate** by spores and division.

C. dubia, E. Australia, 5ft (1.5m) 40°F (5°C).

C. macrocarpa, SW Europe, Atlantic islands, 12–36in. (30–90cm), 40°F (5°C).

Cyathea, from Gr. 'kyatheion', a small cup, a reference to the shape of the indusium; 40 species, American tropics. **Habitat** – steep slopes and ravines in cloud or rain forests; large fern, erect trunk-forming rhizome. **Cultivation** – pots and beds in moist free-draining soil. **Propagate** by spores.

C. arborea, West Indian tree fern, fronds 6–10ft (1.8–3m), trunk 30–50ft (9–15.2m), 60°F (16°C).

C. australis, E. Australia, fronds 14ft (4m), trunk 40ft (12m), 60°F (16°C).

C. cooperi, tropical and subtropical Australia, fronds 20ft (6m), trunk to 40ft (12m), 50°F (10°C).

C. cunninghamii, E. Australia, N.Z., fronds 3–10ft (0.9–3m), trunk to 70ft (21m), 50°F (10°C).

C. dealbata syn. *Alsophila tricolor*, silver tree fern, N.Z., fronds 3–9ft (0.9–2.7m), trunk 30ft (9m), 50°F (10°C).

C. leichardtiana, E. Australia, fronds 10ft (3m), trunk to 22ft (6.7m), 50°F (10°C).

C. medullaris, black tree fern, Sago fern, N.Z., 35–60ft (10–18m), fronds 9ft (2.7m), 50°F (10°C).

C. rebeccae, Australia (Queensland), fronds to 10ft (3m), trunk 30ft (9m), 60°F (16°C).

Cyrtomium, 20 species, tropics and subtropics. **Habitat** – forests, ravines, rocky places and moist cliffs; ascending rhizome. **Cultivation** – containers and rock gardens in free-draining, rocky soil. **Propagate** by spores and division.

C. Fortunei, E. Asia, 12–24in. (30–60cm), 40°F (5°C).

C. caryotideum, E. Asia, 12–24in. (30–60cm), 40°F (5°C).

C. falcatum, Japanese holly fern, E. Asia, 30in. (76cm), 40°F (5°C).

Cystopteris, from Gr. 'kystis', a bag, and 'pteris', a fern, an allusion to the sack-like covering of the sori; 6 species, northern temperate regions and subtropics. **Habitat** – rocky stream valleys and thickets; small fern, decumbent rhizome. **Cultivation** – beds or terrarium in permanently shaded sites in alkaline soil. **Propagate** by spores and division.

C. alpina syn. *C. regia*, Europe, 5in. (15cm), hardy.
C. bulbifera, bladder fern, N. America, 24–36in. (60–90cm), 40°F (5°C).
C. dickieana, Europe, 2–5in. (5–15cm), hardy.
C. fragilis, brittle bladder fern, n&s temperate regions including N. America, 10in. (25cm), hardy.
C. montana, N. America, 6–18in. (16–46cm), hardy.
C. regia syn. *C. alpina*, Europe, 5in. (15cm), hardy.

Davallia, named after Edmund Davall, A Swiss botanist, 40 species, SW Europe, tropical and subtropical Asia and Pacific. **Habitat** – epiphytic and rupestrian; small/medium fern, creeping rhizome. **Cultivation** – baskets sited in indirect light with free-draining, acid soil kept dry between watering. **Propagate** by spores and division. Grown for their attractive scale-clad rhizomes. Fronds shed once a year.

D. canariensis, hare's foot fern, Atlantic islands, SW Europe, 12–18in. (30–46cm), 40°F (5°C).
D. divaricata, S. China, Burma, Malaysia, 3–4ft (.9–1.2m), 60°F (16°C).
D. fejeensis, rabbit's foot fern, Polynesia, 6–12in. (16–30cm), 50°F (10°C).
D. mariesii, ball fern, Japan, China, 6–12in.(16–30cm), 40°F (5°C).
D. pyxidata, E. Australia, 3ft (91cm), 40°F (5°C).
D. solida, SE Asia to Polynesia, 18–36in. (46–91cm), 50°F (10°C).
D. trichomanoides, Japan to Sri Lanka and Malaysia, 10–18in. (25–46cm), 40°F (5°C).

Dennstaedtia, 45 species, pantropics, subtropics and N. America, 3 in temperate America. **Habitat** – wet mountain forest, rocky slopes and meadows; medium/large fern, creeping rhizome. **Cultivation** – open beds in moist, acid soil. **Propagate** by spores and division.

D. cicutaria, common cup fern, C. America, 3–4ft (0.9–1.2m), 50°F (10°C).
D. punctilobula, hay-scented fern, N. America, 18–30in. (46–76cm), hardy.

Dicksonia, named after the English botanist J. Dickson, 20 species, tropical America and Australasia. **Habitat** – steep slopes in cloud forest, in ravines and along streambanks; erect, trunk-forming rhizome. **Cultivation** – open beds and containers in free-draining, acid soil. **Propagate** by spores and offsets.

D. antarctica, soft tree fern, S&E Australia, Tasmania, 35–50ft (10–15m), fronds 6ft (1.8m), 40°F (5°C).
D. fibrosa, N.Z., 12ft (3.6m), fronds 4ft (1.2m), 50°F (10°C), slow growing.
D. squarrosa, N.Z., 10ft (3m), fronds to 4ft (1.2m), 50°F (10°C).

Diplazium, 300 species, tropics and temperate regions. **Habitat** – wet forests, ravines and rocky slopes; medium/large fern, erect rhizome. **Cultivation** – indirect light, moist, well-drained, rich soil. **Propagate** by spores, division and bulbils on *D. proliferum*.

D. esculentum, India to Polynesia, 1–2ft (30–61cm) stems, fronds 2–6ft (0.6–1.8m), 60°F (16°C).
D. proliferum, old world tropics, 1–2ft (30–61cm) stems, fronds 2–6ft (0.6–1.8m), 60°F (16°C).

Doodia, named after the English botanist Samuel Doody (1656–1706); 10 species, Polynesia, Australia, and Sri Lanka. **Habitat** – moist wooded slopes and streambanks; small/medium fern, creeping rhizome, **Cultivation** – terrarium with free-draining, moist/dry soil. **Propagate** by spores. Related to *Blechnum*. Attractive red foliage of young fronds.

D. aspera, rasp fern, E. Australia, 12–16in. (30–41cm), 40°F (5°C).
D. caudata, E. Australia, 4–10in. (10–25cm), 40°F (5°C).
D. maxima, rasp fern, E. Australia, 15in. (38cm), 40°F (5°C).
D. media, rasp fern, Australasia, 8–12in (20–30cm), 40°F (5°C).

Doryopteris, 25 species, tropical America. **Habitat** – moist rocky places, cliffs, boulders and walls; medium fern, creeping rhizome. **Cultivation** – strong light, moist, free-draining alkaline soil. **Propagate** by spores and by buds on *D. pedata palmata*. Species have a wide variation of frond architecture.

D. concolor, Australia (Queensland), 5in. (15cm), 60°F (16°C).
D. ludens, India to N. Australia (Queensland), 3–4in. (7–10cm), barren fronds, 12in. (30cm), fertile fronds, 60°F (16°C).
D. noblis, West Indies, S. America to Peru and Brazil, 4–9in. (10–23cm), 60°F (16°C).
D. pedata, spear-leaved fern, West Indies, tropical America to Argentina, 9in. (23cm), 50°F (10°C).
D. sagittifolia, tropical S. America, 12in. (30cm), 60°F (16°C).

Drymoglossum, 6 species, tropics, **Habitat** – epiphytic on branches, boulders and rocks; small fern, creeping rhizome. **Cultivation** – as *Polypodium*. **Propagate** by spores and division.

D. piloselloides syn. *D. heterophyllum* & *Lemmaphyllum heterophyllum*, India to New Guinea, 4in. (10cm), 60°F (16°C).

Drynaria, 20 species, tropical Asia. **Habitat** – epiphytic, related to *Polypodium*; large, evergreen fern, creeping rhizome. **Cultivation** – in pans and baskets with coarse, organic, moist/dry soil. **Propagate** by spores and division. Attractive oak-leaf fronds.

D. quercifolia, oak-leaf fern, India to Australasia & Polynesia, barren fronds 12in., fertile fronds 36in. (91cm), 60°F (16°C).

D. ridigula, India, S. China, Malaysia to Polynesia and Australia (Queensland), 9in. (23cm) barren fronds, fertile fronds 2–3ft (61–91cm), 60°F (10°C).

Dryopteris, 150 species, 25 in American tropics. **Habitat** – wet forests, ravines, shaded slopes; medium/large fern, ascending/erect rhizome. **Cultivation** – beds and containers in well-drained, slightly acid soil. **Propagate** by spores and division. Fast growing, easily cultivated.

D. aemula, hay-scented buckler fern, Atlantic islands, W. Europe, 6–24in. (16–60cm), hardy.

D. affinis, golden-scaled male fern, Europe to Himalayas, 8–30in (20–76cm), hardy, several subspecies.

D. arguta, coastal wood fern, N. America, 36in. (91cm), evergreen, hardy.

D. atrata, China, 30in. (76cm), 40°F (5°C).

D. austriaca syn. *D. dilatata*, N. America, N. Europe, N. Asia, 36in. (91cm), hardy.

D. carthusiana, narrow buckler fern, Europe, 24in. (60cm), hardy.

D. clintoniana, Clinton's fern, N. America, 48in. (1.2m), evergreen, 40°F (5°C).

D. cristata, crested shield fern, fen-buckler fern, C. Europe to Siberia, N. America, 6–24in. (16–60cm), hardy.

D. dentata, tropics, subtropics, NZ, 36in. (91cm), 50°F (10°C).

D. x deweveri, hybrid narrow buckler fern, 36in. (91cm), hardy.

D. dilatata, broad buckler fern, Europe, 36in. (91cm), hardy.

D. erythrosora, Japanese red shield fern, Japan, China, 10–24in. (25–60cm), hardy.

D. expansa, northern buckler fern, N. Eurasia, N. America, 8–30in. (20–76cm), hardy.

D. filix-mas, common male fern, Europe, N. America, 12–48in. (0.3–1.2m), hardy.

D. fragrans, fragrant shield fern, sub-Antarctic to N. Urals, N. Japan and N. America, 4–10in. (10–25cm), hardy.

D. goldiana, giant wood fern, N. America, evergreen, 4ft (1.2m), 40°F (5°C).

D. x mantoniae, hybrid mountain male fern, 36in. (91cm), hardy.

D. marginalis, marginal shield fern, N. America, 10–30in. (25–76cm), hardy.

D. oreades, mountain male fern, Europe, especially North, 12–18in. (30–46cm), hardy.

D. parallelogramma, tropical America, 36in. (91cm), 50°F (10°C).

D. sieboldii, Japan, 12in. (30cm), 40°F (5°C).

D. submontana, limestone buckler fern, Europe, 36in. (91cm), hardy.

D. wallichiana, Himalayas, 36in. (91cm), hardy.

Elaphoglossum, 400 species, tropics and subtropics (American tropics 350 species). **Habitat** – epiphytic or terrestrial in wet forests; small/medium fern, creeping rhizome. **Cultivation** strong light, very free-draining soil. Slow growing, seldom cultivated. **Propagate** by spores and division.

E. crinitum, elephant's ear fern, West Indies, 8–12in. (20–30cm), 60°F (16°C).

E. petiolatum, SE Asia, 8–16in. (20–41cm), 60°F (16°C).

Equisetum, from Latin 'equus', a horse, and 'seta', bristle, the plant resembling horses' tails; 23 species, worldwide. **Habitat** – bogs, lakes, open sterile soil; medium fern, creeping rhizome. **Cultivation** – invasive, cultivate only in pots. **Propagate** by spores and division.

E. hyemale, Dutch rush, temperate regions, 36in. (91cm), hardy.

E. telmateia, temperate regions, 36–72in. (0.9–1.8m), hardy.

E. variegatum, variegated horsetail, temperate regions, 6–24in. (16–60cm), hardy.

Goniophlebium, from Gr. 'gonia', an angle, and 'phleps', a vein, a reference to the veins on the fronds; 20 species, Asian tropics. **Habitat** – epiphytic; medium/large fern, creeping rhizome. **Cultivation** – epiphytic, treat as *Polypodium*, in baskets with very free-draining soil. **Propagate** by spores and division.

G. subauriculatum, tropical Asia and Australia, 36in. (91cm), 60°F (16°C).

G. verrucosum, Indonesia and tropical Australia, 36in. (91cm), 60°F (16°C).

Gymnocarpium, 2 species, temperate regions.
Habitat – rocky woods; small/medium fern, creeping rhizome. **Cultivation** – shaded areas as ground cover or rockeries in free-draining soil. **Propagate** by spores and division. *G. robertianum* needs an alkaline soil, long lived, fast growing.

G. dryopteris, oak fern, world wide including N. America, 9in. (23cm), hardy.

G. robertianum, limestone oak fern, world wide including N. America, calcareous soil, 15in. (38cm), hardy.

Gymnopteris, 5 species, tropics. **Habitat** – epiphytic; medium fern, creeping rhizome. **Cultivation** – bright, open, well-drained soil. **Propagate** by spores. Related to *Hemionitis*. Dislikes wet conditions.

G. rufa, tropical America, 8in. (20cm), 60°F (16°C).

Hemionitis, from Gr. 'hemionos', a mule, the species being regarded as barren; 6 species, tropical America. **Habitat** – streambanks, rock walls; small fern, ascending rhizome. **Cultivation** – open, bright conditions, free-draining, gritty soil. Dislikes wet, stagnant conditions. **Propagate** by spores and by plantlets on *H. palmata*.

H. arifolia, tropical Asia, 12in. (30cm), stems, fronds 5in. (15cm), 60°F (16°C).

H. palmata, strawberry fern, tropical America, 5–6in. (15–16cm), 60°F (16°C).

Histiopteris, 4 species, tropics. **Habitat** – open woodlands in upland areas; medium/large fern, creeping rhizome. **Cultivation** – strong light, damp, sandy soil. **Propagate** by spores. Fast growing. Treat as *Pteris*.

H. incisa, bat's wing fern, tropics, 24–36in. (60–91cm), 60°F (16°C).

Humata, 50 species, Polynesia, Japan, Himalayas, Malaysia, Madagascar. **Habitat** – epiphytic; small/medium fern, creeping rhizome. **Cultivation** – baskets in free-draining, gritty soil. **Propagate** by spores and division. Slow growing.

H. heterophylla, Indonesia (Sumatra) to Polynesia, 9in. (23cm), 60°F (16°C).

H. pectinata, Indonesia (Sumatra), to New Guinea & Australia, 8in. (20cm), 60°F (16°C).

H. repens, Mascarene islands to N. India, Japan, Malaysia and Australia, 8in. (20cm), 60°F (16°C).

H. tyermannii, hare's foot fern, Himalayas, China, 9in. (23cm), 50°F (10°C).

Hymenophyllum, from Gr. 'hymen', a membrane,

and 'phyllon', a leaf, a reference to the thinness of the fronds; 300 species, worldwide. **Habitat** – terrestrial and epiphytic along streambanks and in wet, shady places; small fern, creeping rhizome. **Cultivation** – as semi-aquatic in terrarium and poolsides with low light and high humidity (90%+). **Propagate** by division.

H. demissum, filmy fern, N.Z., 1–9in. (2–23cm), 40°F (5°C).

H. tunbridgense, Europe, 2–6in. (5–16cm), 40°F (5°C).

H. wilsonii, Wilson's filmy-fern (one-sided filmy fern), Europe, 2–6in. (5–16cm), 40°F (5°C).

Hypolepis, 45 species, tropics. **Habitat** – wet, open areas, clearings and fields; medium/large fern, creeping rhizome; **Cultivation** – indirect light, moist, well-drained soil. **Propagate** by spores and division.

H. millefolium, N.Z., 6–15in. (16–38cm), 40°F (5°C).

H. punctata, pantropics; 3–4ft (0.9–1.2m), 50°F (10°C).

H. repens, bramble fern, tropical America, 3–4ft (0.9–1.2m), 50°F (10°C).

H. rugulosa, temperate S. Hemisphere, 30in. (76cm), 40°F (5°C).

H. tenuifolia, C. Japan to Australia and N.Z., 36in. (91cm), 40°F (5°C).

Lastreopsis, 25 species, tropics. **Habitat** – streamside and ravines; medium fern, creeping rhizome. **Cultivation** – lightly shaded beds or pots in moist, well-drained soil. **Propagate** by spores and division.

L. decomposita, E. Australia (Queensland to N.S. Wales), 36in. (91cm), 50°F (10°C).

L. hispida, E. Australia, Tasmania, N.Z., 40in. (1.2m), 40°F (5°C).

Lemmaphyllum, 4 species, East Asia. **Habitat** – epiphytic; small fern, creeping rhizome. **Cultivation** as epiphyte in baskets or terrarium. Treat as *Polypodium*, **Propagate** by spores and division.

L. microphyllum, E. Asia, 2–4in. (5–10cm), 40°F (5°C).

Leptopteris, from Gr. 'leptos', slender, and 'pteris', a fern; 6 species, temperate regions. **Habitat** – swamps, bogs and lake margins; medium fern, erect rhizome. **Cultivation** – low light, free-draining, moist, acid soil and high humidity. **Propagate** by spores. Related to *Osmunda*. Sow spores within three weeks.

L. hymenophylloides syn. *Todea hymenophylloides*, New Zealand crêpe fern, N.Z., 40in. (1.2m), 40°F (5°C).

L. superba, Prince of Wales' feather, N.Z., 30in. (76cm), 40°F (5°C).

Leucostegia, 2 species, tropical Asia. **Habitat** – epiphytic; medium fern, creeping rhizome.

Cultivation – in baskets with well-drained, dryish soil. **Propagate** by spores and division. Related to *Davallia*.

L. immersa, tropical SE Asia to New Guinea, 24–30in. (60–70cm), 60°F (16°C).

Lindsaea, 150 species, pantropical. **Habitat** – wet or moist forests and marshes. In America in low rain forests, thickets, exposed rocky sites; small fern, erect rhizome. **Cultivation** strong light, poor soil/clay. **Propagate** by spores.

L. linearis, Australasia, 4–8in. (10–20cm), 40°F (5°C).

Lunathyrium, 30 species, tropics. **Habitat** – wet forests; small fern, creeping rhizome. **Cultivation** – deep shade, rocky, moist, acidic soil. **Propagate** by spores. Related to *Diplazium*.

L. japonicum, Japan, SE Asia, Australasia, Polynesia, 12in. (30cm), 40°F (5°C).

Lygodium, from G. 'lygodes', flexible, referring to the twining stems; 40 species, tropics and subtropics. **Habitat** – open forests and the borders of streams; small/medium fern, creeping rhizome. **Cultivation** – bright, filtered sunlight, in peaty soil. **Propagate** by spores.

L. articulatum, N.Z., pinnules 4in. (10cm), 40°F (5°C).

L. flexuosum, S. China, Malaysia, pinnules 8–12in. (20–30cm) long, 6–12in. (15–30cm) broad, 60°F (16°C).

L. japonicum, Japanese climbing fern, India, China, Japan, Korea to Australia, pinnules 4–8in. (10–20cm), 40°F (5°C).

L. microphyllum, tropical Africa, Asia, Australia, pinnules 4–8in. (10–20cm), 60°F (16°C), variety of *L. scandens*.

L. palmatum, Hartford fern/climbing fern, Eastern America, Florida to N. Carolina, pinnules 1–2in. (2–5cm), 40°F (5°C).

L. scandens, tropical E. Asia, pinnules 4–8in. (10–20cm), 60°F (16°C).

Macrothelypteris, 1 species, Pacific. **Habitat** – wet forests; large fern, creeping rhizome. **Cultivation** – bright light, rocky, well-drained soil. **Propagate** by spores. Fast growing.

M. torresiana, Mascarene islands, SE Asia to Japan and Polynesia, 6ft (1.8m), 60°F (16°C).

Marattia, 40 species, tropics. **Habitat** – streambanks and wet ravines. **Cultivation** – damp, acid soil; medium/large fern, erect rhizome. **Propagate** by spores.

M. fraxinea, Australia (Queensland), 6ft (1.8m), 60°F (16°C).

Marsilea, named after the Italian botanist Giovanni Marsiglia; 60 species, worldwide. **Habitat** – shallow water of pools, canals and ditches; small fern, creeping rhizome. **Cultivation** – as aquatic, in pots submerged in water or mud. **Propagate** by spores and division. Easy, slow growing.

M. Drummondii, Australia, stipes 1–2in. (2.5–5cm), 60°F (16°C).

M. fimbriata, tropical W. Africa, stipes 6in. (16cm), leaflets ½in. (1cm), 60°F (16°C).

M. hirsuta, Australia, stipes to 6in. (16cm), leaflets ½in. (1cm), 40°F (5°C).

M. mutica, Australia, stipes to 4in. (10cm), leaflets 1½in. (3cm), 50°F (10°C).

M. quadrifolia, nardoo plant. Eurasia, N. America, stipes 3–6in. (7–16cm), leaflets 1in. (2cm), hardy.

Matteuccia, 2 species, n. temperate regions. **Habitat** – wet or moist shady places; medium/large fern, erect rhizome. **Cultivation** – open shade, moist, neutral soil. **Propagate** by spores and division. Sow spores immediately.

M. pensylvanica, N. America, 3–5ft (0.9–1.5m), hardy.

M. struthiopteris, ostrich feather fern, Europe, 3–5ft. (0.9–1.5m), hardy.

Merinthosorus, 1 species, Malaysia, Solomon islands. **Habitat** – epiphytic; large fern, creeping rhizome. **Cultivation** – as epiphyte in baskets with moist, dry soil. **Propagate** by spores.

M. drynarioides, Malaysia to Solomon Islands, 12in. (30cm), 60°F (16°C).

Microgramma, from Gr. 'mikros', small, and 'gramma', a line, reference to the indusium; 13 species, American tropics. **Habitat** – epiphytic in swamp forests and cloud forests along streams; small fern, creeping rhizome. **Cultivation** – in baskets as for *Polypodium*. **Propagate** by spores and division.

M. vacciniifolia, Brazil, 60°F (16°C).

Microlepia, from Gr. 'mikros', small, and 'lepis', a scale, a reference to the spore cases; 45 species, tropics and subtropics. **Habitat** – ravines and alongside streams in wet forests; medium/large fern, creeping rhizome. **Cultivation** – bright light in beds and pots with well-drained soil. **Propagate** by spores.

M. platyphylla, India, 2–3ft (61–91cm), 50°F (10°C).

M. speluncae, SE Asia to Australia, 3–6ft (0.9–1.8m), 60°F (16°C), evergreen.

M. strigosa, N. India to Japan and Polynesia, 1–3ft (30–91cm), 60°F (16°C), evergreen.

Microsorium, 60 species, small/medium/large fern,

tropics. **Habitat** – epiphytic or aquatic of rivers and swamps; creeping rhizome. **Cultivation** – in baskets with very free-draining soil. **Propagate** by spores and division.

M. musifolium, Malaysia to New Guinea, 4ft (1.2m), 60°F (16°C).

M. pteropus, India, S. China, Malaysia, 16in. (41cm), 60°F (16°C).

M. punctatum, tropical Australasia, Pacific islands, 4ft (1.2m), 60°F (16°C).

M. scandens, E. Australia, 16in. (41cm), 40°F (5°C).

Nephrolepis, from Gr. 'nephros', a kidney, and 'lepis', a scale, a reference to the shape of the indusium; 20 species, tropics. **Habitat** – epiphytic or rupestral on boulders in rain forests, grasslands, open areas and swamps; medium/large fern, erect rhizome. **Cultivation** – epiphytic, and in baskets as underplanting, good light, low humidity, well-drained soil. **Propagate** by spores, division and stolons. Easily grown.

N. acuminata syn. *M. davalloiodes*, Asian tropics including Sumatra, to 6ft (1.8m), 60°F (16°C).

B. biserrata syn. *N. acuta*, tropical America, to 6ft (1.8m), 60°F (16°C), vars. include *N. b. furcans*.

N. cordifolia syn. *N. tuberosa*, fishbone fern, tropics and subtropics including Japan and N.Z., 15–30in. (38–76cm), 50°F (10°C), vars. include *N. c. compacta* and *N. c. tessellata* syn. *N. c. plumosa*.

N. exaltata, swordfern, tropical America, Africa and Polynesia, to 5ft (1.5m), 50°F (10°C), vars. include *N. e. bostoniensis* (Boston fern), *N. e.* 'Ostrich Plume', *N. e.* 'Verona', *N. e.* 'New York', *N. e. Rosseveltii*, *N. e. gretnia*, *N. e. muscosa*, *N. e. scholzelii*, *N. e. scottii*, *N. e. smithii*, *N. e. vistori*, *N. e. wagneri*, *N. e. wicheri*, *N. e.* 'Anna Foster', *N. e.* 'Colorado', *N. e.* 'Fluffy Ruffles' and *N. e.* 'Trevillian'.

N. hirsutula, tropical SE Asia to Pacific, to 6ft (1.8m), 50°F (10°C).

N. pectinata, tropical America, 4ft (1.2m), 50°F (10°C).

N. radicans syn. *N. volubilis*, tropical Asia, 2ft (60cm), 50°F (10°C).

Notholaena, 60 species, worldwide. **Habitat** – in forested areas on boulders and cliffs, in grassland and dry scrub; small fern, creeping rhizome. **Cultivation** – sunny site, very free-draining, rocky or sandy soil. **Propagate** by spores. Long lived, slow growing.

N. marantae, C&S Europe, Atlantic islands, Ethiopia, Himalayas, 4–15in. (10–38cm), hardy.

N. vellea, Mediterranean and Atlantic islands, SW Asia to Afghanistan, 3–10in. (7–25cm), hardy.

Oleandra, 40 species, tropical America, Asia.

Habitat – rupestral in wet forests on tree stumps and trunks and among boulders in acid substrates; medium fern, creeping rhizome. **Cultivation** – as epiphyte in baskets with very free-draining soil. **Propagate** by spores and division. Attractive scaley rhizomes.

O. articulata, SE Asian tropics, 12in. (30cm), 60°F (16°C).

Onoclea, 1 species, temperate. **Habitat** – marshes, swamps and wet woods; medium fern, creeping rhizome. **Cultivation** – bog, streamside and wet soils. **Propagate** by spores and division. Sow spores immediately.

O. sensibilis, sensitive fern, Western N. America, E. Asia, naturalized in parts of Europe, 8–18in. (20–46cm), hardy.

Onychium, from Gr. 'onychion', a small nail, a reference to the shape of the fertile fronds; 7 species, tropics and subtropics. **Habitat** – rocks and dry areas; medium fern, creeping rhizome. **Cultivation** – light shade, beds and pots with moist soil. **Propagate** by spores and division. Fast growing, valued for delicate foliage.

O. japonicum, Japan, China, 8–24in. (20–60cm), 40°F (5°C).

Ophioglossum, 30 species, world-wide. **Habitat** – open soil or grasslands; small/medium fern, creeping rhizome. **Cultivation** – shaded sites in damp, neutral soil. **Propagate** by division. Long lived, slow growing. Unpredictable in cultivation.

O. pedulum, old world tropics, 6in. (16cm), 60°F (16°C).

O. vulgatum, adder's tongue, worldwide, 6in. (16cm), hardy.

Oreopteris, from Gr. 'oros', a mountain, and 'pteris', a fern; temperate Europe. **Habitat** – upland wet areas, related to *Thelypteris*. **Cultivation** – beds and borders with wet, acid soil. **Propagate** by spores and division.

O. limbosperma, sweet mountain fern, N. Europe, 36in. (91cm), hardy.

Osmunda, 10 species, worldwide. **Habitat** – swamps, bogs and lake margins; large fern, erect rhizome. **Cultivation** – moist, acid soil alongside pools. **Propagate** by spores and division. Sow spores immediately.

O. cinnamomea, cinnamon fern, eastern N. America and tropical America, 5ft (1.5m), hardy.

O. Claytoniana, interrupted fern, eastern N. America, 4ft (1.2m), hardy.

O. regalis, royal fern, widespread in temperate and subtropics, 4ft (1.2m), hardy, cultivars include *O. r.*

cristata and *O. r.* purpurascens.

Paesia, 12 species, pan-tropics. **Habitat** – rocky woods; small/medium fern, creeping rhizome. **Cultivation** – light shade, free-drained, moist soil. **Propagate** by spores and division.

P. scaberula, N.Z., 9–24in. (23–60cm), 40°F (5°C).

Pellaea, from Gr. 'pellos', dark hue, a reference to the colour of the stipes; 35 species, pantropical and temperate regions. **Habitat** – open rocky places, cliffs and dry woods; creeping rhizome. **Cultivation** – beds and pots, in good light, in well-drained alkaline soil. **Propagate** by spores and division.

P. atropurpurea, purple rock brake, America, from Canada to Mexico, alkaline soil, 12–18in. (30–46cm), 40°F (5°C), evergreen, tolerates full sun.
P. brachyptera, California. 4–6in. (10–16cm), 50°F (10°C).
P. falcata, Australian rock brake, Australia, 12–18in. (30–46cm), 50°F (10°C).
P. rotundifolia, button fern, N.Z., 6–18in. (16–46cm), 50°F (10°C).
P. viridis, green rock brace, Africa, Mascarene islands, 24in. (60cm), 50°F (10°C).

Phegopteris, temperate Europe, N. America and Asia. **Habitat** – moist, shady, rocky woods and gullies; small fern, creeping rhizome. **Cultivation** – shady rockeries and borders, in moist free-draining gritty soil. **Propagate** by spores and division. Related to *Thelypteris*.

P. connectilis, beech fern, temperate Europe and Asia, 12in. (30cm), hardy.
P. decursive-pinnata, Japan, Taiwan, 8–24in. (20–60cm), hardy.

Phlebodium, from Gr. 'phlebos', a vein, and 'odus', a tooth; 3 species. **Habitat** – epiphytic; creeping rhizome. **Cultivation** – in baskets, strong light, well-drained soil. **Propagate** by spores and division. Related to *Polypodium*.

P. aureum, syn. *Polypodium aureum*, tropical America, 5ft (1.5m), 50°F (10°C).

Phyllitis, 4 species, n. temperate regions. **Habitat** – damp forests and hedgebanks; medium fern, ascending rhizome. **Cultivation** – sheltered, moist, well-drained alkaline soil. **Propagate** by spores, division and basal cuttings. Fast growing.

P. sagittata, Mediterranean, 12in. (30cm), 40°F (5°C).
P. scolopendrium, Europe, 24in. (60cm), hardy, many varieties.

Phymatodes, 10 species, tropical Asia. **Habitat** – terrestrial, rupestral, epiphytic; small fern, creeping rhizome. **Cultivation** – in baskets, as *Polypodium*. **Propagate** by spores and division.

P. diversifolia, E. Australia, N.Z., 24in. (60cm), 50°F (10°C).
P. nigrescens, Malaysia, Polynesia, 6ft (1.8m), 60°F (16°C).
P. scolopendrina, tropical Asia, 18in. (46cm), 60°F (16°C).

Pilularia, from Latin 'pilula', a pill, a reference to the round spore cases; 6 species, wide distribution. **Habitat** – wetlands, marshes and watercourses; small fern, creeping rhizome. **Cultivation** – aquatic, in mud-filled pans. **Propagate** by division.

P. globulifera, W. Europe, 4in. (10cm), hardy.

Pityrogramma, 40 species, Africa, American tropics. **Habitat** – rocky banks and cliffs; small fern, ascending rhizome. **Cultivation** – bright light and dry air in baskets with sandy, moist/dry soil. Avoid wetting fronds. **Propagate** by spores. Short lived, fast growing. Prefers dry conditions, good frond colour.

P. argentea, American goldback fern, 24–36in. (60–91cm), 40°F (5°C).
P. calomelanos, silver fern, tropical America, old world tropics, Pacific and Australia, 3ft (91cm), 50°F (10°C).
P. chrysophylla, gold fern, S. America and old world tropics, 12–24in. (30–60cm), 40°F (5°C), vars. include subs. *P. c. heyderi* and *P. c. farinifera*.
P. hybrida = *P. chrysophylla* x *P. calomelanos*, 24in. (60cm), 40°F (5°C).
P. Pearcei syn. *P. decomposita*, Peru, 12in. (30cm), 60°F (16°C).
P. pulchella, Venezuela, 12in. (30cm), 60°F (16°C).
P. sulphurea, Jamaica, 12in. (30cm), 60°F (16°C).
P. tararea subs. *P. t. aurata*, tropical America, 12–24in. (30–60cm), 60°F (16°C).
P. triangularis, California gold fern, California to Mexico, 15in. (38cm), 40°F (6°C), vars. include *P. t. viscosa*, *P. t. pallida* and *P. t. maxonii*.

Platycerium, from Gr. 'platys', broad, and 'keras', a horn, an allusion to the shape of the fronds; 15 species, tropics. **Habitat** – epiphytic in rain forests; large fern. **Cultivation** – strong light, walls, baskets in peat/moss compost. **Propagate** by spores and offsets.

P. andinum, Bolivia and Peru, 6–9ft (1.8–2.7m), 60°F (16°C).
P. angolense, elephant's ear fern, 3ft (91cm), 60°F (16°C).
P. bifurcatum, many subsp., stag's horn fern, Australia

(Queensland and New South Wales), 36in. (91cm), 50°F (10°C), many varieties.

P. coronarium, Thailand, Malaysia, 24in. (60cm), 60°F (16°C).

P. grande, N. Australia, 4ft (1.2m), 50°F (10°C).

P. hillii, Australia (N. Queensland), 4ft (1.2m), 60°F (16°C).

P. stemmaria, Africa, 18in. (46cm), 60°F (16°C).

P. superbum, Australia (Queensland New S. Wales), 24in. (60cm), 60°F (16°C).

P. vassei, Africa, Madagascar, 12–24in. (30–60cm), 60°F (16°C).

P. veitchii, Australia (C&N Queensland), 24in. (60cm), 40°F (5°C).

P. willinckii, Java, 4ft (1.2m), 60°F (16°C).

Pleopeltis, 40 species, tropics. **Habitat** – epiphyte of rain forests; large fern, creeping rhizome. **Cultivation** – in baskets, as for *Polypodium*. **Propagate** by spores and division.

P. crassifolium, West Indies, Mexico, Brazil, 36in. (91cm), 60°F (16°C).

P. phyllitidis, tropical America, 36in. (91cm), 60°F (16°C).

Polypodium, from Gr. 'polys', many, and 'pous', a foot, a reference to the creeping rhizomes; 75 species, widespread incl. temperate and tropical regions. **Habitat** – low epiphyte on trees, rocks and rotted wood; medium fern, creeping rhizome. **Cultivation** – on rocks, indoor baskets or terrarium with moist, free-draining soil. **Propagate** by spores and division.

P. angustifolium, tropical America, 12–18in. (30–45cm), 60°F (16°C).

P. aureum, golden polypody, subtropical and tropical America, 24-36in. (60–91cm), 50°F (10°C).

P. australe, southern polypody, Europe, 12in. (30cm), hardy.

P. azoricum, Azores, 4–12in. (10–30cm), 40°F (5°C).

P. brasiliense, tropical S. America, 18–30in. (46–76cm), 60°F (16°C).

P. californicum, syn. *P. intermedium/P.V. intermedium*, California, 4–12in. (10–30cm), 60°F (16°C).

P. cambricum, Europe, 5–12in. (15–30cm), hardy.

P. coronans, India, 12–36in. (30–91cm), 60°F (16°C).

P. crassifolium, W. Indies, 12–36in. (30–91cm), 60°F (16°C).

P. fimbriatum, S. America, 6–16in. (16–41cm), 60°F (16°C).

P. glycyrrhiza, liquorice fern, N. America, 4–12in. (10–30cm), 40°F (5°C).

P. hesperium, N. America, 8in. (20cm), 40°F (50°C).

P. interjectum, western polypody, W. Europe, 6–16in. (16–41cm), hardy.

P. lepidopteris, S. America, 24in. (60cm), 60°F (16°C).

P. loriceum, W. Indies, 18–24in. (46–60cm), 60°F (16°C).

P. lycopodioides, tropical America, 2–4in. (5–10cm), 60°F (16°C).

P. macaronesicum, SW Europe, Madeira, Canary islands, 4–15in. (10–38cm), 40°F (5°C).

P. maritimum, C. America, 12–24in. (30–60cm), 60°F (16°C).

P. meniscifolium, Brazil, 12–30in. (30–76cm), 60°F (16°C).

P. pectinatum, Brazil, 18–30in. (46–76cm), 60°F (16°C).

P. plebejum, tropical America, 6–18in. (16–46cm), 60°F (16°C).

P. polycarpon, tropical Asia, 12–36in. (31–91cm), 60°F (16°C).

P. polypodioides, resurrection fern, subtropical and temperate America, acid soil, 2–10in. (5–25cm), 40°F (5°C).

P. ptilorhizon, W. Indies, 6–12in. (16–30cm), 60°F (16°C).

P. rhodopleuron, C. America, 9–16in. (23–41cm), 60°F (16°C).

P. scouleri, leather fern, Pacific coast of N. America, 6–24in. (16–60cm), hardy.

P. sub-auriculum subs. *P. s. knightiae*, Asia, Australia, 3–4ft (0.9–1.2m), 60°F (16°C).

P. thyssanolepis, C. America, 4–12in. (10–30cm), 60°F (16°C).

P. triseriale, S. America, 12–24in. (30–60cm), 60°F (16°C).

P. virginianum, N. America, 10in. (25cm), 40°F (5°C).

P. vulgare, common polypody, Eurasia, N. America, 3–16in. (7–14cm), hardy.

Polystichum, from Gr. 'polys', many, and 'stichos', a row, a reference to the sori; 160 species, worldwide. **Habitat** – mountainous regions, ravines and stream banks; small/medium/large fern, ascending/erect rhizome. **Cultivation** – shaded, sheltered site, some species prefer an alkaline soil, well drained. **Propagate** by spores, division and bulbils.

P. acrostichoides, Christmas fern/dagger fern, eastern N. America, 12–30in. (30–76cm), hardy.

P. aculeatum, hard shield fern, n. temperate Eurasia, 12–36in. (30–91cm), hardy.

P. adiantifolium syn. *P. adiantiforme*, S. America, 12–36in. (30–91cm), 40°F (5°C).

P. aristum, Australasia, 12–24in. (30–60cm), 40°F (5°C).

P. braunii, N. America, temperate Europe, 12–36in. (30–91cm), hardy.

P. californicum, California, 1–4ft (0.3–1.2m), 50°F (10°C).

P. cystosterigia, N.Z., 8–18in. (20–46cm), 40°F (5°C).

P. dudleyi, California, 1–4ft (0.3–1.2m), 50°F (10°C).

P. lonchitis, holly fern, Europe and N. America, alkaline soil, 8–24in. (20–60cm), hardy.

P. luctosum, Africa, 1–3ft (30–91cm), 60°F (16°C).

P. munitum, western sword fern/giant holly fern, western N. America, alkaline soil, 18–36in. (46–91cm), hardy.

P. setiferum, soft shield fern, Atlantic islands and W. Europe, 12–24in. (30–60cm), hardy, many varieties.

P. tripteron, Japan and area, 24in. (60cm), 40°F (5°C).

P. tsus-simense, warm temperate Asia, 8–18in. (20–46cm), hardy.

P. vestitum, N.Z., fronds 12–36in. (30–91cm), trunk to 5ft (1.5m) hardy.

Pteris, 200 species, tropics and subtropics. **Habitat** – rocks, walls, clearings in woods and rocky stream banks; small/medium/large fern. **Cultivation** – bright, filtered sunlight, high humidity, well-drained acidic soil. **Propagate** by spores.

P. argyrea, Sri Lanka, Java, 12–36in. (30–91cm), 60°F (16°C).

P. biaurita, tropics, 6–12in. (16–30cm), 40°F (5°C).

P. comans, Australasia, Polynesia, 12in. (30cm), 60°F (16°C).

P. cretica, ribbon fern, tropics and sub tropics, 6–36in. (16–91cm), 40°F (5°C), many varieties.

P. dispar, tropical Asia, 6–10in. (16–25cm), 50°F (10°C).

P. ensiformis, sword brake fern, Himalaya, Australia (Queensland), Polynesia, 12in. (30cm), 50°F (10°C), many varieties.

P. faurei, China, 12–18in. (30–46cm), 60°F (16°C).

P. multifida, spider fern, Japan, China, 12–36in. (30–91cm), 40°F (5°C).

P. paradoxa, E. Australia, 12in. (30cm), 40°F (6°C).

P. quadriaurita, India, Sri Lanka, 12–18in. (30–46cm), 60°F (16°C).

P. semipinnata, SE Asia, Japan, 12–18in. (30–46cm), 50°F (10°C).

P. serrulata, Canary Islands, SW Europe, N. Africa, Arabia, 3–5ft (0.9–1.5m), 50°F (10°C).

P. ternifolia, C&S America to Argentina and N. Chile, 6–18in. (16–46cm), 40°F (5°C).

P. tremula, table fern, Australasia, 4ft (1.2m), 60°F (16°C).

P. tripartita, Japan, 60°F (16°C).

P. umbrosa, E. Australia, 12–18in. (30–46cm), 60°F (16°C).

P. viridis, Africa, Mascarene islands, 24in. (60cm), 50°F (10°C).

P. vittata, Japan, 24in. (60cm), 40°F (5°C).

Pyrrosia, 100 species, NE Asia and temperate areas. **Habitat** – epiphytic; medium fern, creeping rhizome. **Cultivation** – in baskets, humid areas with good light and very free draining soil. Needs frost-free area for outdoor cultivation. **Propagate** by spores and division. Related to *Polypodium*.

P. angustata, Malaysia, 5–12in. (15–30cm), 60°F (16°C).

P. beddomeana, China, 12–30in. (30–76cm), 60°F (16°C).

P. confluens, Australasia, 4–10in. (10–25cm), 50°F (10°C).

P. hastata, Japan, 12in. (30cm), 50°F (10°C).

P. heteractis, East Indies, 4–7in. (10–18cm), 60°F (16°C).

P. lingua, felt fern, S. Japan, 4–10in. (10–25cm), 40°F (5°C), many cultivars.

P. longifolia Malaysia, Australia, 8–24in. (20–60cm), 50°F (10°C).

P. macrocarpa, Asia, 4–10in. (10–25cm), 60°F (16°C).

P. nummularia, Himalayas to Philippine islands, 2–4in. (5–10cm), 60°F (16°C).

P. piloselloides, Asia, 30in. (76cm), 60°F (16°C).

P. polydactilis, Taiwan, 12in. (30cm), 60°F (16°C).

P. rupestris, E. Australia, 1–3in. (2–7cm), 40°F (5°C).

P. samarensis, Asia, 6–18in. (16–46cm), 50°F (10°C).

P. serpens, Australia, (Queensland), 2–6in. (5–16cm), 60°F (16°C).

P. varia, New Guinea, 8in. (20cm), 60°F (16°C).

Quercifilix, 1 species, Asiatic tropics; small fern, ascending rhizome. **Cultivation** – in pots with very free-draining, sandy soil. **Propagate** by spores. Related to *Tectaria*.

Q. zeylanica, Mauritius, Sri Lanka, S. China, Taiwan, Malaya, Borneo, 2in. (5cm), 60°F (16°C).

Regnellidium, 1 species, Brazil. **Habitat** – aquatic in stagnant pools; small fern, creeping rhizome. **Cultivation** – submerged in water, or in mud-filled pans. **Propagate** by division.

R. diphyllum, S. Brazil, 4in. (10cm), 60°F (16°C).

Rumohra, 2–6 species, tropics or southern hemisphere. **Habitat** – open, sandy soil in shrubby areas and on rocks; medium fern, creeping rhizome. **Cultivation** – as terrestial or epiphyte, strong screened light, free-draining, gritty soil. **Propagate** by spores and division.

R. adiantiformis, leather fern, southern hemisphere, 12–36in. (30–91cm), 60°F (16°C).

Sadleria, 6 species, Pacific Islands; large fern, erect, trunk-forming rhizome. **Cultivation** – strong, filtered sunlight, free-draining, moist soil. **Propagate** by spores. Slow growing, seldom grown. Related to *Blechnum*.

S. cyatheoides, Hawaii, 36in. (91cm), 60°F (16°C).

Salvinia, named after the Florentine botanist, Salvini; 10 species, temperate America and Africa. **Habitat** – lakes, rivers, ditches and ponds; small fern, creeping rhizome. **Cultivation** aquatic, needs strong or slightly filtered light. **Propagate** by division.

S. auriculata, tropical America, 1in. (2cm), 60°F (16°C).

S. minima, water spangles, 1in. (2cm), 50°F (10°C).

S. natans, tropical Asia and Africa, 4in. (10cm), 60°F (16°C).

Schizaea, 30 species, tropical and warm temperate regions. **Habitat** – lowland clay soils; medium fern, creeping or erect rhizome. **Cultivation** in beds, in base, dryish soil. **Propagate** by spores.

S. fistulosa, N.Z., 2–10in. (5–25cm), 40°F (5°C).

S. pusilla, curly grass fern, Eastern N. America, 2–4in. (5–10cm), 40°F (5°C).

Scyphularia, 8 species, New Guinea to Malaysia. **Habitat** – epiphytic; small/medium fern, creeping rhizome. **Cultivation** – in baskets with a free-draining, gritty soil. **Propagate** by spores.

S. pentaphylla, Indonesia to New Guinea, 12in. (30cm), 60°F (16°C).

Selaginella, 800 species, worldwide. **Habitat** – wide range of habitats, wet rocks to xeric scrub; medium fern. **Cultivation** – as terrestial in pots or epiphyte in baskets. **Propagate** by spores and division.

S. apoda syn. *S. apus*, N. America, 1–4in. (2.5–10cm), 50°F (10°C).

S. kraussiana, Azores and Africa, 6in. (16cm), 50°F (10°C).

S. plantaginea, SE Asia, Polynesia, 5in. (15cm), 60°F (16°C).

S. selaginoides syn. *S. spinosa*, Europe, N. America, 2–3in. (5–7.6cm), hardy.

Sphenomeris, 20 species, tropics. **Habitat** – rocks and scrub; medium fern, erect rhizome. **Cultivation** – gritty, well-drained soil.

S. chusana, E. & SE Asia to Madagascar and Polynesia, 24–30in. (60–76cm), 50°F (10°C).

Stenochlaena, 40 species, Malaysia, Africa. **Habitat** – terrestrial or epiphytic in wet woods; large fern, creeping rhizome. **Cultivation** – baskets in moist soil. **Propagate** by spores and division. Fast growing.

S. palustris, Malaysia to Polynesia, 16–30in. (41–76cm), 60°F (16°C).

S. tenuifolia, tropical Africa, Madagascar, 12–24in. (30–60cm), 60°F (16°C).

Tectaria, 200 species, pantropical. **Habitat** – wet forest, streambanks and forest slopes, some on limestone; medium/large fern, ascending/erect rhizome. **Cultivation** – in pots, tubs and beds with a moist soil. Needs high humidity. **Propagate** by spores and division.

T. cicutaria, button fern, West Indies, 30in. (76cm), 60°F (16°C).

T. decurrens, Polynesia, 24in. (60cm), 60°F (16°C).

T. heracleifolia, West Indies, C. America to Peru, 36in. (91cm), 60°F (16°C).

T. incisa, Mexico, West Indies to Brazil, 36in. (91cm), 60°F (16°C).

T. macrodonta, Malaysia, Philippine islands, Solomon islands, Fiji, 36in. (91cm), 60°F (16°C).

T. subtriphylla, India, Taiwan, 24in. (60cm), 60°F (16°C).

Thelypteris, 800 species, worldwide. **Habitat** – wet places; medium fern, erect rhizome. **Cultivation** – part shade, moist, neutral-to-acid soil. **Propagate** by spores and division. Fast growing, short lived, good foliage.

T. acuminata, Japan, 6in. (16cm), 40°F (5°C).

T. decursive-pinnata, Japan, 36in. (91cm), 40°F (5°C).

T. dentata, tropical Asia, 36in. (91cm), 60°F (16°C).

T. hexagonoptera, broad beech fern, N. America, 12–30in. (30–76cm), 40°F (5°C).

T. nevadensis, N. America, 18–36in. (46–91cm), 40°F (5°C).

T. normalis, SE America, 24–36in. (60–91cm), 50°F (10°C).

T. noveboracencis, New York fern, N. America, 36in. (91cm), hardy.

T. ovata, Himalayas, 6–12in. (16–30cm), 50°F (10°C).

T. palustris, marsh fern, Europe, Asia, N. America, 12–36in. (30–91cm), hardy.

T. parasitica, tropical Asia, 36in. (91cm), 60°F (16°C).

T. patens, tropical America, 24–36in. (60–91cm), 60°F (16°C).

T. phegopteris, syn. *Phegopteris connectilis*, northern beech fern, N. America, 12in. (30cm), hardy.

T. puberula, California, 36in. (91cm), 50°F (10°C).

T. quadrangularis, tropical America, 36in. (91cm), 60°F (16°C).

T. simulata, N. America, 12in. (30cm), 40°F (5°C).

T. torresiana, tropical America, 48in. (1.2m), 60°F (16°C).

Thyrsopteris, 1 species, Juan Fernandez Islands (tropical America). **Habitat** – upper woodlands; medium fern, erect rhizome. **Cultivation** – warm, humid, light shade, moist, humus-rich soil, well drained. Make small trees. Treat as *Dicksonia*. **Propagate** by spores.

T. elegans, Chile, 5ft (1.5m), 60°F (16°C).

Todea, named after the German botanist, Henry James Tode; 2 species, South Africa, Australia, N.Z. **Habitat** – lowland forest, scrub and open, rocky places; medium fern, ascending rhizome. **Cultivation** – moist sites, near water, less hardy than Osmunda. **Propagate** by spores and division.

T. barbara, Prince of Wales' feather, S. Africa, E. Australia, N.Z., 4ft (1.2m), caudex 2ft (61cm), 40°F (5°C).

Trichomanes, from Gr. 'thrix', a hair, and 'manos', soft, an allusion to the surface of the fronds; 300 species, pantropical, subtropical and temperate regions. **Habitat** – wet rocks, some species epiphytic; small fern, creeping rhizome. **Cultivation** needs 100 per cent humidity, suited to terrariums. **Propagate** by division.

T. Boschianum, N. America, 8in. (20cm), 40°F (5°C).

T. Petersii, Eastern N. America, 5in. (15cm), 40°F (5°C).

T. speciosum, syn. *T. radicans*, Killarney fern, cup goldilocks, Europe and N. America, 6in. (16cm), 40°F (5°C).

Vittaria, 50 species, tropics and subtropics. **Habitat** – epiphytic on rotting wood, boulders and rocks in rain forests; small/medium/large fern, creeping rhizome. **Cultivation** – in baskets with a free-draining gritty soil. **Propagate** by spores and division.

V. elongata, Malaysia to Australia, 12–24in. (30–60cm), 60°F (16°C).

V. scolopendrina, S. Africa and Malaya, 12in. (30cm), 60°F (16°C).

Woodsia, named after the English botanist, Joseph Woods, 25 species, alpine, boreal and temperate regions. **Habitat** – shrubby hillsides, on ledges, boulders, stone walls and rocky soils; small fern, erect rhizome. **Cultivation** rock gardens, terrarium, open-textured soils. **Propagate** by spores and division.

W. alpina syn. *W. hyperborea*, alpine woodsia, N. America, N. Europe, 2–6in. (5–16cm), hardy.

W. glabella, N. America, alkaline soil, 2–6in. (5–16cm), hardy.

W. ilvensis, oblong woodsia, N. America, N. Europe, rock crevices, acid soil, 2–8in. (5–20cm), hardy.

W. obtusa, N. America, neutral soil, 10–16in. (25–41cm), hardy.

W. oregana, N. America, 5–9in. (15–23cm), hardy, varieties include *W. o. cathcartiana*.

W. scopulina, N. America, 7–18in. (18–46cm), hardy, varieties include subs. *W. s. appalachia*.

Woodwardia, named after the English botanist T.J. Woodward; 10 species, Europe, Asia, N. America. **Habitat** – forest areas alongside streams, moist meadows and damp, rocky places; medium/large fern, creeping, erect or ascending rhizome. **Cultivation** – most prefer some shade, *W. Virginica* will tolerate full sun in well drained, permanently moist acid soil. **Propagate** by spores and division. Vigorous growth.

W. areolata, netted chain fern, N. America, 12–30in. (30–76cm), 50°F (10°C).

W. fimbriata syn. *W. chamissoi*/*W. radicans americana*, N. America, 3–6ft (0.9–1.8m), 50°F (10°C).

W. japonica syn. *W. radicans japonica*, Japan, 36in. (91cm), 50°F (10°C).

W. orientalis syn. *W. radicans orientalis*, China, Japan, Taiwan, 12–48in. (0.3–1.2m), 50°F (10°C).

W. radicans, Asia, SW Europe, 2–6ft (0.6–1.8m), hardy.

W. unigemmata syn. *W. radicans unigemmata*, China, Japan, Taiwan, 2–6ft (0.6–1.8m), hardy.

W. virginica, Virginia chain fern, N. America, 4ft (1.2m), 40°F (5°C).

GLOSSARY OF TERMS

Acid	Soil with a pH below 7.0.
Alkaline	Soil with a pH above 7.0.
Antheridium	The mechanisms producing the male cells.
Apex	The tip of a frond.
Apogamous	Reproduction from prothalli without fertilization.
Apospory	Formation of prothalli on the frond without the intervention of spores.
Aquatic	Growing on or below water.
Archegonium	The structure within which the female egg is produced.
Axis	Central part of the frond about which the blade is arranged.
Bigeneric	A hybrid derived from two different genera.
Bipinnafid	Twice pinnafid.
Bipinnate	Twice pinnate; both primary and secondary divisions of the frond are pinnate.
Blade	The leafy part of a frond.
Bulbils	Buds which form on the fronds of some viviparous ferns.
Calcifuge	Lime hating.
Capitate	Possessing a terminal crest.
Circinate	The unfolding of the fronds.
Cordate	Heart-shaped.
Cretinate	Fronds having scalloped margins.
Cuneate	Wedge-shaped.
Deciduous	Annual shedding of seasonal growth.
Decumbent	Horizontal to the ground, with growing tip ascending.
Deflexed	Turning downwards.
Deltoid	Triangular
Denticulate	Teeth-like margins.
Dimorphic	Possessing both vegetative and fertile fronds.
Entire	Undivided
Epiphyte	A fern adapted to growing on mossy rocks or branches of trees.
Family	A group composed of related genera.
Fimbriate	Fringed margins.
Flushing	Initial growth at the start of the season.
Gametophyte	The prothallus. The sexual stage in the fern cycle.
Genus (pl. genera)	A group of related species.
Habitat	The natural location of a plant.
Hardy	Ability to survive frost in open ground.
Hybrid	The offspring from two different species or varieties.
Indusium	A membrane protecting the sorus.
Lanceolate	Lance-shaped, broadest at the base and tapering towards the end.

Linear	Long and narrow.
Marginate	Deeply frilled margin.
Ovate	Egg-shaped.
Palmate	Hand shaped.
Pinna	The first major division of the fern frond.
Pinnate	With leaflets on each side of the midrib, in herringbone fashion.
Pinnatifid	Almost divided to the midrib.
Pinnule	One of the divisions of a pinnae, i.e. a secondary division of the frond.
Prothallus	A small disc-like plant, the gametophyte generation of a fern, arising from the germination of a spore.
Rachis	The central midrib of the frond.
Reflexed	Bent backwards or downwards.
Rhizome	Rootlike stem emitting roots and fronds.
Rupestral	Growing on boulders and rocky outcrops.
Sagitate	Arrow-shaped.
Scandent	Sprawling growth over low branches and scrub.
Serrate	With edges saw-toothed.
Simple	Undivided.
Sorus	A cluster of sporangia.
Spinose	Bearing spines.
Sporangia	Spore-bearing structures.
Spore	A minute reproductive cell.
Sporophyte	The spore-producing form in the fern life cycle.
Stipe	The stalk of the frond.
Stolon	Prostrate, creeping stem giving rise to a further plantlet, as in *Nephrolepis* species.
Terrestial	Growing in the soil.
Tripinnate	Three separate divisions of the frond.
Undulate	With a wavy edge or margin.
Venation	Arrangement of the veins in a blade.
Viviparous	Producing plantlets as buds or bulbils on fronds, as in *Asplenium bulbiferum*.

FERN GARDENS

Ferns are a feature in many gardens which are open to the public. The following gardens, however, have particularly good collections of ferns. For anyone who wishes to cultivate these diverse and adaptable plants much valuable experience can be gained by visiting these gardens.

Dundee University Botanic Garden,
Riverside Walk, Dundee, Scotland.
A newly-developed garden, it features a large conservatory housing a range of hardy and tender ferns, including *Dicksonia*, *Lygodium*, *Platycerium* and *Woodwardia* species. A particular feature of this garden are the natural effects created in the planting of epiphytic, scandent and aquatic ferns.

Glasgow Botanic Garden,
Great Western Road, Glasgow, Scotland.
One of the oldest botanic gardens, founded in 1818, it has an impressive range of tropical and subtropical ferns. The Kibble Palace houses the British national collection of *Dicksonia*, numbering some 100 *D. antactica* and *D. squarrosa*. The extensive collection of New Zealand species of *Trichomanes* and *Hymenophyllum* within the Filmy Fern House is internationally renowned. A recent plant hunting expedition to Papua New Guinea returned with a large number of epiphytic ferns.

Harlow Car Gardens,
Cragg Lane, Harrogate, Yorkshire.
Within the grounds of The Northern Horticultural Society can be found one of the finest collections of European and N. American hardy ferns.

Royal Botanic Gardens, Kew,
Kew Road, Richmond, Surrey.
Kew hosts one of the finest collections of tender ferns from around the world.

Royal Botanic Garden, Edinburgh,
Inverleith Road, Edinburgh.
One large house is given over to tender and semi-tender ferns. Here can be found *Dicksonia*, *Woodwardia* and many low-growing ferns in an imaginative, indoor waterside rock garden.

Saville Gardens,
The Great Park, Windsor.
This beautifully landscaped garden features many hardy woodland and waterside ferns.

Sizergh Castle,
Sedgewick, nr. Kendal, Cumbria.
Waterside and woodland ferns abound in this small garden. A feature of the garden is the wealth of varieties of *Phyllitis scolopendrium*, *Polypodium*, *Polystichum* and *Dryopteris* species. Along with Harlow Car, Sizergh Castle holds the national collection of British hardy ferns.

Free University of Amsterdam Botanic Garden,
Van der Boechorstraat 8, 1081 BT Amsterdam, Holland.
Sited on a small island, the botanic garden is host to many fine, old varieties of hardy ferns, cultivated within a small, woodland setting. The garden has a large collection of tender ferns under glass, with the main emphasis on *Asplenium*. A smaller alpine house has a good collection of *Adiantum* species.

University of Berkeley Botanic Garden,
Berkeley, California.
The 25 acres of garden and 8 greenhouses are host to a large collection of ferns from temperate and tropical regions.

Brooklyn Botanic Gardens and Arboretum,
New York.
This garden has a good collection of tender ferns under glass.

Garfield Park Conservatory,
N. Central Park, Chicago 24, Illinois.
The garden houses a collection of tropical ferns under glass.

Eden Park Conservatory,
Cincinnati 2, Ohio.
Tender ferns of the tropics feature in this garden.

Caribbean Gardens,
Naples, Florida.
This private garden open to the public has a good collection of tropical ferns.

Fairchild Tropical Gardens,
Old Cutler Road, Miami 56, Florida.
The large garden of 86 acres is host to many species of sub-tropical ferns.

Other fern gardens in the USA

Alabama:	Haleyville, Natural Bridge Park.
	Bama Scenic Rock Garden, Vance.
California:	Patric's Point, Stagecoach Hill.
	Rosecroft Begonia Gardens, San Diego.
Carolina:	Elizabethan Garden, Manteo.
	Sarah Dukes Garden, Durham. (Hugo L. Blomquist Collection).

Florida:	Univ. of South Florida Botanic Gardens, Tampa.
	Miami Beach Garden Centre, Miami Beach.
	Marie Selby Botanic Garden, Sarasota.
Hawaii:	Kalopa, Hawaii.
Indiana:	Hayes Regional Arboretum, Richmond, Indiana 47374.
Maine:	Rockland.
	Woolwich.
Massachusetts:	Alexander Botanic Garden, Wellesley College, Wellesley. (Hawaiian ferns).
	Garden in the Woods, South Sudbury, (New England Wild Flower Society's collection of native species of ferns and varieties).
New Hampshire:	Lost River, Nature Garden.
Ohio:	Krohn Conservatory, Cincinnati.
Oregon:	Louis Simpson Estate, Charlestown.
Pennsylvania:	Bowman's Hill Wild Flower Preserve, Washington Crossing State Park.
	Longwood Gardens, Kennet Square, Pennsylvania 19348.

FERN SOCIETIES

The British Pteridological Society
c/o Dept of Botany, British Museum (Natural History),
Cromwell Road, London SW7 5BD.

The British Pteridological Society was formed in 1891. Originally titled The Northern Pteridological Society, it owed its origin to Robert Whiteside, a keen fern collector living in the English Lake district. On the demise of an earlier London-based society, it took up its present title.

Members receive two journals per annum. *The Pteridologist*, a forum for gardeners and amateur naturalists interested in ferns and their allies, and *The Fern Gazette*, of specialized interest, and mainly dealing with fern taxonomy.

The society operates a spore exchange network, and organizes field trips to venues of interest to members.

The American Fern Society,
c/o Dept. of Botany, University of Vermont,
Burlington, Vermont.

Founded in 1893, the society publishes two quarterlies, *Fiddlehead Forum*, a journal catering to the general fern enthusiast, and *The American Fern Journal*, a more academic journal mainly dealing with taxonomic issues.

The society operates a spore distribution network for its members. Regional societies undertake field trips to sites of pteridological interest.

ANTIQUARIAN BOOKS

Bosanquet, Revd Edwin *A Plain Account of British Ferns* 1854.

Bower, F.O. *The Ferns* 1923, 3 vols, Camb.

Britten, J. *European Ferns* 1878.

Heath, F.G. *The Fern World* 1898.

Hibbert, James Shirley *The Fern Garden* 1869.

Hooker, Sir William Jackson, *British Ferns* 1861.

Francis, George William *A Catalogue of British Flowering Plants and Ferns* 1835.

Lowe, E.J. *British and Exotic Ferns* 1856.

Lowe, E.J. *Fern Growing* 1895.

Moore, T. *The Ferns of Britain and Ireland* 1855. Later edition entitled *Nature Printed British Ferns* 1859, 2 vols, London.

Moore, T. *British Ferns and their Allies* 1881.

Moore, T. *A Popular History of British Ferns* 1851.

Newman, E. *A History of British Ferns and Allied Plants* 1844.

Plues, Margaret *Rambles in Search of Flowerless Plants* 1864.

Riley, John *A Catalogue of Ferns* 1841.

Smith, John *British and Foreign Cultivated Ferns* 1857.

BIBLIOGRAPHY

Allen, D.E. *The Victorian Fern Craze* 1969, Hutchinson.

Allen, H.H. *The Flora of New Zealand*, vol. 1, 1961, N.Z.

Chitterden, F.J. *Royal Horticultural Society Dictionary of Gardening* 1977, Oxford.

Cobb, Broughton *A Field Guide to Ferns* 1946 Riverside Press, Cambs., Mass.

Clapham, A.R., Tutin, T.G. & Warburg *Flora of the British Isles* 1952/57/59, Cambs. Univ. Press.

Copeland, E.B. *Genera Filicum* 1947, Waltham, Mass.

Cranfill, R. *Ferns and Fern Allies of Kentucky* 1980.

Dunbar, Lin *Ferns of the Coastal Plain* 1989.

Duncan, Betty D. & Golda Isaac *Ferns and Allied Plants of Victoria, Tasmania and South Australia* 1986.

Everett, Thomas H. *New York Botanic Garden Illustrated Encyclopedia of Horticulture* 1981, Garland Publishing, NY.

Foster, F.G. *The Garden Fern Book* 1965, Nostrand, NY.

Foster, F.C. *Ferns to Know and Grow* 1971, Hawthorne Books, NY.

Frankel, E. *Ferns, A Natural History* 1981, Steven Green Press.

Franks, W. *Platycerium – Fern Facts* 1969, Los Angeles.

Grillos, S.J. *Ferns and Fern Allies of California* 1966, Univ. of Calif. Press.

Hallowell, Anne C. & Hallowell Barbara G. *Fern Finder: A guide to Native Ferns of the Northeastern and Central North America* 1981.

Hoshizaki, B.J. *The Fern Growers Manual* 1975, Knopf, NY.

Hyde, H.A. & Wade, A.E. *Welsh Ferns* 1954, Cardiff.

Jalas, J. and Suominem, J. *Atlas Florae Europaeae, Pteridophyta* 1969, Helsinki.

Jermy, A.C. et al *Atlas of Ferns of the British Isles* 1978.

Kaye, R. *Hardy Ferns* 1968, Faber and Faber, London.

Key, S.J. *Field Guide to Missouri Ferns* 1982.

Lellinger, D.B. *A Field Manual of the Ferns & Fern Allies of the United States and Canada* 1985, Smithsonian Inst. Press.

Lellinger, D.B. *The Ferns and Fern Allies of Costa Rica, Panama and the Choco* 1989.

Mickel, J.T. *Ferns and Fern Allies* 1979, Wm. C. Brown, Iowa.

Mickel, J.T. *How to Know Ferns and their Allies* Reinhardt, NY.

Mohlenbrock, R.H. *The Illustrated Flora of Illinois: Ferns* 1967.

Ogden, E.C. *Field Guide to Northeastern Ferns* 1981, New York State Museum Guide.

Olson, W.W. *The Fern Dictionary* 1977, Los Angeles Fern Soc.

Page, C.N. *Ferns* 1988, Collins.

Page, C.N. *The ferns of Britain and Ireland* CUP.

Parsons, Francis T. *How to Know the Ferns* 1961, Dover, NY. reprint of 1899.

Phillips, Roger *Grasses, Ferns, Mosses and Lichens* 1980, Ward Lock.

Proctor, G.R. *Ferns of Jamaica* 1985.

Rush, R. *A Guide to Hardy Ferns* 1984, British Pterological Society.

Snyder, L.H. & Bruce J.G. *Field Guide to the Ferns and other Pteridophytes of Georgia* 1986.

Taylor, Peter *British Ferns and Mosses* 1960, Eyre and Spottiswoode.

Taylor, W.C. *Arkansas Ferns and Fern Allies* 1984.

Thieret, J.W. *Louisiana Ferns and Fern Allies* 1980, Univ. of S. Louisiana.

Tryon, R.M. & A.F. *Ferns and Allied Plants with special reference to tropical America* 1982, Springer Verlag.

Tryon, R. *Ferns of Minnesota* 1980.

Walters, S.M. et al *The European Garden Flora vol 1* 1986, CUP.

Wharton, Mary E. & Barbour, Roger *The Wild Flowers and Ferns of Kentucky* 1971, University Press of Kentucky.

Wherry, E.T. *The Fern Guide* (North East and Mid. USA) 1961, Doubleday, NY.

Wherry, E.T. *The Southern Fern Guide* (SE and S. Mid. USA) 1965, Doubleday NY.

Willis, J.C. *A Dictionary of Flowering Plants and Ferns* 1966, CUP.

INDEX

GENERAL

PLANT